My Liberated Life

Thecla E. McCarthy

PublishAmerica
Baltimore

First printing

ISBN: 1-60703-373-9
PUBLISHED BY PUBLISHAMERICA, LLLP
www.publishamerica.com
Baltimore

Printed in the United States of America

This book is dedicated to
The Holy Family
Jesus, Mary, Joseph

Acknowledgments

"When the risen Lord appears to the Apostles on Easter, the first thing he does is show them his hands. Because the risen Lord is still the crucified Lord his action says, 'See how much I love you.' The Church's teachings are often dismissed as mean-spirited. In reality they are a road map to a life of love, a wholly human life, A LIBERATED LIFE." Cardinal Sean P. O'Malley, OFM cap.

This quote inspired the title of my book. That's how I feel about my life. I am so grateful for the Faith my parents passed on to me, for the people who came into my life through that Faith. This book is my attempt to repay them.

My road map to a life of love led me to a desire to fly in an open-cockpit plane in the '30s, to look into the music world in the '40s, to share my life with my husband and our love of a large family in the '50s, to share our family with families overseas in the '60s and '70s. Later in life, to enjoy exotic honeymoons in Canada and countries in Central America when Terry took short-term contracts to work there. Flying in our small plane through Central America provided vistas of those countries I never saw before—matching the thrill of hearing Rachmaninov's Second Symphony for the first time. Finally, I saw new worlds visiting my children and grandchildren in foreign lands. The open-cockpit flight came when I was eighty.

My deep appreciation to my husband, Terry, who always presented new horizons to me, to my children, Terry Jr., Kevin, Rory, Robert, Cronan, Sean, Christopher, Brigid, Hilary, Camille, who always rose to the occasion, to Joseph and Mary, our intercessors in heaven, to Sue, Micki, Amy, Nancy, Tina, Dotty, Gina, Brian, Laura and Duane for adding their love to our family, to our grandchildren and great-grandchildren who never cease to amaze me with their skills.

I gratefully acknowledge the insights written by Rory, Cronan, Bob and Hilary included in the book.

Brigid and Camille's quilt of our family provided the cover of the book—the quilt was presented to Terry and me at our fiftieth wedding anniversary reunion in 2000.

Our profession in the Secular Franciscan Order gave us spiritual brothers and sisters all over the world—they are with us to this day.

My sincere thanks to my mentor, Penny Porter, for her encouragement; to Terry Sr. and Terry Jr., who put up with my lack of knowledge of computers; to my readers, Sue McCarthy and Barbara Trent, and to my grandson, Rob McCarthy, who designed the cover.

About the Cover: McCarthy Family Quilt

Our daughter Camille made a family quilt for our fiftieth wedding anniversary. Her sister Brigid collaborated with her—they decided on the quilt since we requested that no gifts be given.

Brigid, who lives in Arizona, brought our wedding photos with her when she visited Camille in North Dakota. Together, they chose the fabric for the quilt. Camille admitted the most difficult part was obtaining the current family photos from her brothers—these were photocopied onto fabric making up the squares of the quilt.

They are arranged in the age of the children from left to right: Top row, Terry Jr., Kevin and Rory; second row, Bob, our wedding photo in 1950 and Cronan (David and Mary, deceased, were added to the photo); third row, Sean, our photo at Hilary's wedding and Christopher; fourth row, Brigid (Kolbe was added to the family just before the reunion), Hilary and Camille.

There are two little angels between our wedding pictures crocheted by Ilene Williams, a neighbor of Bob and Nancy—they represent Joseph and Mary, our two children who died as infants.

What a wonderful gift—the family, our treasure!

Table of Contents

Chapter I

That Old Feeling

"They want you to go *where?*"

"To Suriname—it's a country on the northern tip of South America: former Dutch Guyana."

I turned from the stove, sat down at the table with Terry, and wondered what this was all about.

"Suriname—I don't remember ever hearing of that country let alone going there. Why has Texas A&M asked you to go there?"

"Actually, Alcoa wants me to go there—Suralco, a subsidiary of Alcoa, has a bauxite mine there. They were interested in hiring a student from the Heavy Equipment Training Program here at A&M to train men at the bauxite mine in Suriname."

"How did you get involved in this?"

"Well, a while back, Elmer Brenn, from the main office of Alcoa in Pittsburgh, sent a letter regarding this to Alvin Jones here at the Engineering Extension Service. Alvin handed the letter on to me—when I read it, I decided to send my resume in as well as the students' resumes."

"You mean, when Mr. Brenn came here last week to interview the students, he decided he wanted you?"

"That's what happened—Alcoa is looking for the same kind of training in Suriname that I did for the Agency for International Development in Costa Rica when we lived there."

"Does Alcoa depend that much on the bauxite mined in Suriname?"

"Yeah, they've been mining, processing and exporting bauxite since 1916. In fact, the Dutch Air Force protected the mine during WWII—we were very dependent on it."

"Wow, this is a lot different though than taking our family for this kind of work in Costa Rica—we were pretty much on our own there."

11

"That's true, we did our own thing with reports to the government—now we'll be under a large company with their regulations. Some of our kids are in high school now too—there're questions about the education part that need answering."

"Uh-oh. Would it mean using correspondence courses for the children like we did in Costa Rica?"

"Maybe some—Alcoa maintains an American School in Suriname for grades one through eight—children of high school age are expected to stay in the States for their education: that's the problem."

"High school is too young an age for the children to be away from the family."

"That's for sure—we'll need to check into what correspondence courses are available for them."

"Wonder how the children will like that. Is it a contract for a certain number of years?"

"No, I'd be working for Alcoa there until there are enough local men to take over the training—no time specified."

"Wow, let me think about this for a while."

"Okay, that's what I want you to do."

This challenge fascinated me; I like that feeling—I remembered it when we prepared to go to Costa Rica with the family a few years earlier; in fact, it went back farther than that—a lot farther back.

****

It started in the late 1930s; we didn't see very many planes flying around then. I came home from school for lunch one day, just a regular school day routine; we waited for a few minutes but when my dad didn't appear, we started eating. As we finished the meal, he walked in with a big grin on his face.

Mom said: "You're late, George."

"I just flew in an airplane; look I even burned my arm on the exhaust pipe just below the cockpit: I guess I got too excited and tried to look around to see everything and put my arm down too far."

Mom looked horrified.

"George, how could you do that—you could have been killed—you know I'm afraid of planes."

12

"Flying's the most wonderful feeling in the world: the wind in your face, the fields and town stretched out in all directions. You ought to try it."

"I just don't know how you could do that!"

Too excited to hold back, I said: "Dad, how did you find the plane? There's no place here in town where a plane can land."

"One of the customers came into the shop to get his car repaired and he told me that a barnstormer came to town to give airplane rides to anyone interested. He landed in the pasture just outside of town on Jefferson Street so I went there, and he took me up."

"Did you wear a helmet and goggles? I've seen pictures of the pilots wearing them in those planes."

"You bet I did. That's all part of it."

"That's the most exciting thing I've ever heard. I can't wait to tell everyone at school."

I knew right then that someday I had to fly in a plane like that. Dad didn't go to the airport in St. Louis to fly in a plane—he flew from a pasture just outside of our little town of Washington, Missouri: that's the kind of plane ride I wanted.

That year when Dad took the family on our yearly trip to the St. Louis Zoo, he stopped at Lambert Field on the way home to watch the planes. There I saw people taking rides in a Stearman. They put on a helmet and goggles and took off—just like Dad had done. It looked so wonderful.

"Dad, please let me take a ride in the plane."

"If I let you go, your brothers and sisters will want to take a ride too. I can't afford that."

"None of them want to go. Mom, please tell Dad it's all right."

"It's just too dangerous. I don't want you to go."

From the look on her face I knew it was a lost cause for now. But, there's always next year.

My life went on; in 1941, Dad and a fellow worker repaired a new Hudson which looked completely wrecked but the damage proved superficial: only front end body work was needed—the engine was untouched. Mom, Dad, two sisters, a brother and I took a trip to Fort Pierce, Florida, in it: some of Dad's relatives lived there. We crossed the Ohio River on a ferry, went atop Lookout Mountain in Tennessee where "The Battle above the Clouds" was fought during the Civil War. We then fought our way through the torrential rain of the remnants of a hurricane in Georgia before we saw the Atlantic Ocean in Florida: the sight was well worth it. Looking at the vastness of it all, I wondered about the countries beyond the ocean…would I see them one day?

My second year in high school, WWII started. Here in our little town, quiet and peace reigned, yet the radio and newspapers and the newsreels, shown before the movie started in the theater, told about the fierce battles fought across the oceans. It didn't make sense to me. My dad spent a lot of time talking to me during that time while we sat on the front porch of our home. "We must send our troops overseas to fight so we won't need to fight here on our soil."

"Then why do we have brownouts here with Civil Defense men patrolling the street tonight? Are they expecting a battle here?"

"They just want us to be prepared for anything. We're only fifty miles from St. Louis—there are small-arms factories there. There's an ammunition dump that we pass on Highway 66 when we go to St. Louis. We see guards on horseback patrolling that fenced-in area."

"Well, I feel we aren't doing anything here while our friends and neighbors lose their lives far away. My own brother, Jerry, is in the Navy and my sister, Marcella, in the Army Nurse Corps."

"We need stamps to buy gas and tires for our car; Mom needs stamps to buy food: she can't always get pork or beef so we eat mutton. I ate a lot of mutton when I served in WWI—I really hated it—it had the taste of wet wool. Anyway, that's our part of it now."

During my last two years in high school, much time focused on the ongoing war—life-sized pictures of different battles appeared on the walls of the school library. One picture showed the front line of soldiers coming onshore from a landing craft in one of the battles; a classmate of mine almost fainted when she saw it: there, as big as life, was her brother, leading the group coming onshore.

I worked for a photographer after school during that time: I washed and dried the prints from the rolls of film our customers brought in. Almost all of them were pictures of soldiers on leave with their families and girlfriends and wives.

During my senior year in 1943, the boys in my class gave the nuns teaching us a lot of disciplinary problems. They knew that a few weeks after graduation in June, life in the Armed Forces awaited them. One day I got fed up with all their disruptions and left class and walked home. My dad happened to be home at the time recuperating from recurring problems he suffered with his arm and hand: injuries incurred during WWI.

"What brings you home at this hour of the day?"

"I'm not going back to school; it's a waste of time. The boys in my class disrupt the class so much it's useless."

"They're just thinking too much about going off to war right after graduation: it's hard for them. What do you think you'll accomplish by leaving school?"

"I don't want them wasting my time."

"Who do you think is getting hurt here—the boys or you?"

"Me, I guess."

"Okay, then go back to school—now."

I dreaded going back—walking out of class and out of school with no excuse entailed serious consequences. I reported to Sister Euthalia, in the superior's office: I knew my home room teacher had to report the incident to her. I was in deep trouble! Sister Euthalia gave me permission to return to class under her conditions: many after-school hours writing about school rules and various other subjects as punishment—lost money too for not reporting for work on time at my job.

All thoughts about flying for pleasure left me during that time—planes for the military were the nation's concern then. My first full-time job after graduation was in the office of a shoe factory which manufactured shoes for the men and women in the military. What had been our very ordinary shoe factory took on a military atmosphere, complete with a high barbed-wire-topped fence and a guardhouse out front. We all wore ID badges which the guard checked. Even though the guard had known me all my life, I still had to sit in the guardhouse until identified by my boss when I occasionally forgot my badge.

It was not a happy time: many of my friends and schoolmates did not come home from that war. My friend Mary Beth Jasper's brother was navigator on a fighter plane on an aircraft carrier—their plane was lost in a battle and when his personal belongings arrived back home, his mother never mentally recovered from the shock.

My sister Marcella was an Army nurse stationed in Richland, Washington, at a top-secret project there. My brother Jerry served aboard an old WWI ship, the USS *Vega*, during the last battles in the Pacific.

Then the war ended. I changed jobs and worked in the office of the garage where my dad was a mechanic; it was also the dealership for Hudson cars. We bought a 1946 model: a shortage of materials like chrome for bumpers did not deter sale of the cars. On our car, my brother simply turned a sturdy piece of lumber into a bumper for it. We took a trip to Michigan in this oddly equipped car and received many strange looks and laughs from motorists as we drove down Lakeshore Drive in Chicago on our way.

That was the era of the big bands and how I enjoyed them: Glenn Miller, Harry James, Benny Goodman, Stan Kenton. I especially liked Miller's "Moonlight Serenade" and Kenton's "Mañana" with June Christy singing the lyrics.

A local pianist, Sonny Lefholz, put a very good group of young musicians together who loved jazz, especially Stan Kenton's progressive jazz, and formed an orchestra.

My sister Georgia, my brother Harold and I started singing together during that time. We were part of a large family: singing provided most of our entertainment. Dad taught us to sing in harmony right from the start. Georgia, Harold and I sang without any written music—just in natural harmony. I decided to find someone to write good arrangements for us. This took me to St. Louis where I found one, Ken Schuler. With his arrangements, we started singing weekend performances with the Sonny Lefholz band for a few years when they performed within the area of our town. We enjoyed it. Then Harold went off to college and our trio broke up.

Trio with Sonny Lefholz band

I always wanted to see new things, try new things, to always look for something better. Memories of those times came tumbling back. I loved living in a large family: seven sisters and three brothers. It never got boring. Sometimes I took my younger siblings and neighbor kids on rides after I learned to drive. One street in town offered a nice hump that tickled their tummies when I took my foot off the accelerator at the right time.

Once, when I took them to the St. Louis Zoo, we had a flat tire on Kingshighway, a busy thoroughfare. I never changed a tire before and wondered what I would do. Luckily, the street bordered a part of Forest Park; with the children safely seated on the grass, I opened the trunk. A man approached me just then and asked if I needed help. As I turned to face him, I saw a tow truck parked a little distance behind my car.

"The lady in the truck is my boss, and she said anyone who brings that many children to the park deserves help to change a tire."

While he changed the tire, I walked back to the truck to thank her and to pay for it.

"No, that's my treat for you and the children."

I loved kids; when I looked at them I knew that I wanted children of my own someday who would look into my eyes that special way a child looks up into its mother's eyes

When the pastor of our parish, Father Erwin, asked me to work as a secretary to the parish, I accepted the job. Shortly after that, Dad decided to apply for a job at a Hudson car dealership in St. Louis. I took a day off and went with him.

While he waited to be interviewed, I went downtown to Radio Station KXOK in the Star Times Building: we always listened to the Song and Dance Parade shows of the disc jockey, Rush Hughes. I knew he had a noon show and decided to watch it from the studio. I walked into the newsroom of the *Star Times* newspaper located on the first floor of the building and approached the girl at the first desk.

"Where is the studio where Rush Hughes does his broadcasts?"

"The radio studios are on the third floor."

"Thank you."

I wondered what the studios looked like and how many there were. There's probably a place where I can sit and watch him. I decided to take the elevator to the third floor and find out.

18

Leaving the elevator, I walked into a very quiet and rather dark hallway and found a studio with a large window; I looked inside at a desk with a microphone on it, shelves of records on one wall, and a glassed-in control room at the other end—no one in sight though.

I left and walked down the other end of the hallway. A door marked Studio B with no windows greeted me.

What do I do now? Would I disturb the show in progress? I'll never know if I don't try, so here goes.

I opened the door and felt the vacuum of the space between it and the second door: sound-proofed. I opened the second door and walked inside the studio. Rush Hughes' theme song was playing but no one was sitting at the desk with the microphone. I saw some chairs on the far side of the room and walked in front of the control room to get to them: two engineers stared at me from the control room. I sat down and as the theme song "Knightsbridge March" played on into parts I never heard before, I wondered what happened. Suddenly, I heard the door nudge a little as the outer door apparently opened and, staring at me the whole time, Rush Hughes burst in, made a dive for the desk and switched on the microphone.

A handsome man in his forties, with black hair and dark eyes, broad shoulders and a very commanding presence, Rush opened the show and introduced the record which the engineer then put on the turntable. He switched off his microphone and looked at me again.

"Who are you?"

"I'm Thecla Holtmeyer."

"What was your mother frightened by—a string of pearls?"

"No—that's my name. I listen to your shows at home in Washington. I'm waiting for my dad to finish some business; I decided to catch your noon show."

He chuckled; so we chatted in between the records he played until the end of the half-hour show. After he signed off, he walked over to a table which held a stack of records which apparently came in the mail and looked through them; he handed me some he didn't want.

"How about coming to lunch with me?"

"Okay."

During lunch at a little deli nearby, we talked about various recording artists and records.

"I'm going back to my office now—I still am surprised that your sole purpose of coming here was to watch my show."

"That's it; good-bye and thanks for lunch."

I picked up Dad.

"How did you do, Dad? Get the job?"

"Yeah, I start work in a couple of weeks—they said they'd start me tomorrow if I wanted."

"That's great; but now you'll be driving fifty miles to work every day; I guess I'd better find work here too so we can drive together. Dad, you won't believe where I've been. I went to Rush Hughes' noon show—he took me to lunch afterwards and gave me some records."

"Wait till you tell your sister Georgia that: she's one of his biggest fans."

Dinner waited for us when we returned home. I looked for Georgia and held out my hand to her.

"Shake the hand that shook the hand of Rush Hughes today."

"You're nuts; I heard his noon and 3:00 show so he wasn't at any record store or anything like that."

"I was in the studio during the noon show and what's more, he took me to lunch and gave me these records."

She stared at me.

"You really did, didn't you! Tell me about it—every bit of it."

A few days later, I received a call from Rush's secretary, Kay O'Connell.

"Rush wants to know if you want a job here in his office: you could start anytime."

"I'll think about it and call you later."

That threw me a curve: I didn't know anything about radio work; I liked the secretarial job at my parish. But Dad really needed someone to drive to St. Louis with him.

I talked with the pastor about the new development.

"Thecla, if you want to take that job, it's okay with me. I'll ask Georgia if she wants to work here."

That's what happened: Georgia took over my job and Dad and I started working in St. Louis.

I really enjoyed working for Rush Hughes Radio Features: never a dull moment. Three half-hour shows at 10:00 a.m., 12:00 p.m. and 3:00 p.m., called the *Song and Dance Parade*, featured old and new releases; the 6:00 p.m. show, called *The First Five*, featured the best-sellers for that day at the various stores which I polled each day. I remember one evening while driving home, listening to the six o'clock show, Rush started laughing before he announced the best-seller.

"I just read the note from my secretary in charge of polling the stores; okay, the best seller was the Mills Brothers recording of 'Across the Alley From the Alamo,' but tonight I'll play Stan Kenton's 'Peanut Vendor' instead."

I wrote in the note that I was sorry that I had to do it again but the Mills Brothers' record was tops: I knew he was as tired of playing that as I was—we'd heard it for weeks.

Rush also sent his recorded *Song and Dance Parade* shows to radio stations around the Midwest. At the studio, he recorded his comments on a sixteen-inch, long-play disc and gave the title of the record to be played. Both sides of one of these long-play discs held five days of his comments. The various radio stations had the records he announced and played them at the proper time. I air-mailed these recorded comments each week to the stations. There were days I received a desperate call from a station saying they couldn't get a particular record: off I went to the record distributing house to pick one up and air-mail it to the station.

At times, I went to the recording studio with Rush when he recorded shows: I held the disc above the turntable until he signaled me and then I let it drop to start recording. Other times, I went to the KXOK studio to put on one of his recorded shows if he was unavailable at the time to do the show. He told me not to ever let the engineers at the station know that I never saw the inside of a radio station before I came to work for him. He also told me never to let my voice be heard if the mike was open or we'd have trouble with the broadcasters' union.

A couple of years later, Rush decided to leave St. Louis and went to Florida for work as a sports announcer. Before he left, he introduced me to Richard Christy, the manager of Capitol Records Distributing House in St. Louis: he hired me and I started working there.

While I worked for Rush, I learned that he was a cousin of Howard Hughes and that he worked as a stunt man in Hollywood for a while. He broke both his hands in a fall during that time—that was the reason for the difficulty with his hands that I noticed when I first met him.

Capitol Records provided a difference in lifestyle for me—a much more stressful world. I started out at the counter in the front office; juke box operators came in and listened to new releases in the booths provided. The booths were more or less soundproof but the people using them never bothered to shut the doors when they played the records—the result was a din of noise rather than listening to music. I wrote out the orders for the records and gave them to the shipping department who packaged them for the customers.

The juke box operators from East St. Louis were in a class all their own. I never knew what to expect. If a best-seller was out of stock, there was pandemonium. They always paid for the records in cash and pulled out a fistful of bills and peeled off the amount of their purchase.

On an autumn morning, one of them had a sweater on; he put his hands into the pocket of the sweater as he waited and looked surprised when he pulled out a roll of money.

"Damn, I wondered what happened to that money last spring."

"Must be nice to forget about a roll of money like that," was all I could say in answer to him.

I upgraded to the middle office a little later, where I took phone orders from stores and wrote up the orders the salesmen sent in. I still dealt with irate customers when the best-sellers were out of stock. Mr. Christy did not want to overstock as he felt his predecessor did; consequently, he came up with some far-out excuses for the lack of records. Tension was high at times when our salesmen and some customers tried to get us to fill their back orders before their turn came. The high turnover rate of employees didn't help the situation. I received a gold pin from the Capitol Records' office in Los Angeles when I completed my first year.

The second year there, I occupied a desk in Mr. Christy's office as his secretary. A man, slight in stature, very nervous, always wearing a bow tie, and finding it very difficult to tell the truth, he was quite the opposite in all ways from Rush Hughes. He played jazz guitar and frequently played all-night gigs at jazz spots around the city. He had a very sweet wife who at times called and asked if he came in to work that morning.

One of the perks that came with the job was seeing the artists when they came to the office and going to their concerts; we visited with them backstage during the breaks. Stan Kenton and Nat King Cole were my favorites. Kenton always had great musicians in his band—Maynard Ferguson was really young, about sixteen, at that time. Nat King Cole, a very gracious man, told us: "I like to meet the Capitol people—they're always young and enthusiastic."

A few years passed. On a vacation in Petoskey, Michigan, our friend Father Hugolinus, pastor of the Franciscan church there, offered me a job as secretary of the parish. That presented quite a different way of life again—back to the days before my work with Rush Hughes and now from Capitol Records. I had to think about this.

"Thank you for the offer, Father."

"You can think about it and let me know later—there's no big hurry involved."

"I'll do that."

I liked my work at Capitol Records even though it proved stressful at times. However, working at a parish in northern Michigan presented quite a challenge. If I took this job, I'd leave the music world but have the chance to try a whole new way of life in an entirely new place. Maybe I'd find that man there to share my dreams. *Where was he anyway?*

"I accept your offer, Father. I'll see you in a few weeks."

Mom and Dad did not agree with my decision. I gave Capitol Records my two weeks' notice. In the evenings, I began setting aside things to pack. Mom would hardly look at me.

"I don't want you to go that far away—there are no relatives there. You'll have no family around."

"But, Mom, I want to try something new."

Dad joined in: "You know I always hoped some of the family would make it in the music world—you're leaving the chance to do that."

"Dad, I've seen the artists and talked with them—that's not the kind of life I want."

In the end, Mom and Dad refused to drive me to St. Louis to catch the train taking me to Chicago and on to Petoskey. I hoped they'd see it differently later. Georgia and Harold did the honors and waved good-bye to me at Union Station in St. Louis on a Sunday afternoon.

In Chicago, I changed stations and boarded the Pere Marquette train bound for Petoskey. The car I entered looked like those used in the cowboy movies. Dim electric bulbs replaced the gaslight in the fixtures. The seats offered little comfort for the overnight ride around Lake Michigan and up the Indiana and Michigan shoreline. Sleep overcame the discomfort as the train obediently followed the track to its destination: Grand Rapids and ultimately, Petoskey.

Gray light greeted us at dawn—thick heavy clouds obscured the sun as we moved over the bleak, vacant countryside that first day of November. The train proved to be a milk run and we frequently stopped to pick up cans of milk left alongside the tracks.

I began to wonder if I suffered a lapse of sanity when I accepted this offer. Then I realized that the first of November was All Saints Day and a Holy Day of Obligation—that meant attending Mass. Where would I be able to do that? There were no evening Masses at that time.

The conductor called out Grand Rapids—there would be a two-hour delay before the train completed its run to Petoskey. The man at the ticket counter directed me to a church which was a few blocks from the train station. After Mass, there was time for breakfast before boarding the train again.

At 10:15 a.m., we were on the last leg of our trip to Petoskey. The first few hours passed quickly as the groups of passengers chatted back and forth. Soon there were only a few left in the car with me. Father Hugolinus waited at the station for my arrival. As he greeted me he said: "Have you gone to Mass today?"

"Yes, Father, I went in Grand Rapids."

Chapter II

Anywhere You're Going

Terry walked into the office of St. Francis Xavier Church in Petoskey, Michigan, that certain day in late November of 1948 just as a newly married couple walked out with their marriage certificate in hand.

"Those poor people; I feel sorry for them."

Mm, what am I dealing with here?

"Do you speak from experience?"

"No, and I intend to keep it that way."

He had a very self-assured manner about himself. I noticed his unusual headgear as I looked at his handsome, ruddy-complexioned face and gazed into his very large blue eyes. (I learned later the headgear was made from an Alaskan hair seal.)

"How can I help you?"

"I just wanted to say 'hi' to Father Hugolinus and let him know I'm back from Alaska for a short visit with my mother."

I rang for Father.

"What were you doing in Alaska?"

"I worked for the Alaska Railroad. They were building a bridge across a canyon—I operated the crane setting steel for the bridge."

This must be the Terry McCarthy I noticed when I posted Sunday collections in the book. There were blank spaces behind his name now after being consistently filled in before. When I noticed that at the time I asked Father what had happened to him.

"He belonged to the youth group here and sang in the choir but left to work in Alaska."

He was talking with Father in the office across the hall now and as he was leaving, I heard Father say: "Terry, you're welcome to come to the youth group and sing in the choir until you go to South America to work."

"I might just do that, thank you, Father."

Several days later he did come to choir rehearsal. I sat behind him looking at his head of very black hair—a very interesting person indeed. After rehearsal, my friend Elizabeth and I were walking down the hall. Terry came up behind us.

"Where are you going?"

"Anywhere you're going." I couldn't believe I was saying that. I never said anything like that before to someone I didn't know.

But that's exactly what I did from then on: we were always together.

Petoskey is a beautiful city on the shore of Little Traverse Bay of Lake Michigan. I had spent short summer vacations here with my family. Now, as I was seeing it with Terry, everything was different. Together, we watched the waves, which I had seen so gentle in the summer, now crashing onto the dock, splashing high in the air—a wild beauty. We took long Sunday drives to see the farm he once lived on in East Jordan and see the beautiful lakes in the area.

On one of those drives, a Stearman came into my life again. We were on our way to visit Terry's sister in nearby Harbor Springs. I saw a Stearman on a grass field at a small airport. Wow, just what I wanted. We went in and asked the pilot to take me for a ride.

"It's quite a job to get the radial engine started—I just don't feel like doing that today, sorry."

Terry said: "Maybe I can help you get it started."

"No, I just don't want to fly today."

Nothing we said changed his mind. Once again I had to accept "no" for an answer—I won't give up though. I'll get that flight.

During all this time, I didn't hear a word from Terry about going to South America to work. Instead, he went to work in the boiler room of the *City of Cheboygan*, a ferry that carried cars and passengers across the Straits of Macinac between Lake Michigan and Lake Huron.

He stopped by the office one day on his way to work at the Straits.

"Why don't you come up Sunday and take the trip across the Straits on my last shift?"

"That sounds great. I'd love to do that."

When I arrived at the parking lot by the ferry dock Sunday, I couldn't believe the change in the Straits. In summer, the blue of the water defied description. Now, dark, gray, choppy waves crashed onto the dock. When the ferry came in, the ramp which enables the cars to load and unload was in place but at the last minute, a wave tossed the ferry up and as it came down again, the ramp dropped with a loud bang onto the dock. Before it could be secured, another wave caught it and the process was repeated. After several attempts, the ferry was finally secured.

Terry met me on board and took me down into the boiler room; I watched the fireman shovel coal into the firebox of the boiler. From there, we went into the engine room. I'm usually not bothered by motion sickness but the room was quite warm, the ferry rocked from side to side while the steam engine connecting rods went up and down—that spelled trouble.

"Terry, I'm going up on deck right now."

"Okay, I'll see you there a little later."

When I got outside, the nausea left. I loved the feel of the wind in my face; the gulls looked so different flying against the gray clouds now instead of the blue summer sky.

Later, Terry came up on deck. "Do you feel like having lunch now?"

"That sounds great to me."

We went inside the cabin; I noticed the tablecloths were wetted down to hold the plates in place. There was a wooden rim on the edge of the table which gave added protection. I enjoyed a T-bone steak with all the trimmings: a wonderful day.

As the weeks passed, we watched the Bay slowly filling in with ice as winter set in. I was learning to ice skate on the rink in the natural setting of the beautiful Winter Sports Park. There I was introduced to the "snow jumper," a single runner with a seat on top. With a little run on top of the hill to get you started, you jump onto the seat and balance yourself on the one runner as you fly down the hill. I gave up on that one.

We went to the "Winter Sports Ball"—Governor G. Mennen Williams crowned the Winter Sports Queen that year. Terry gave me a beautiful corsage of camellias which I treasured. They were perfect on the aqua blue velvet gown I wore—my mom made it for me when I was bridesmaid for my sister's wedding the month before I left home.

When the ice took over the water in the Straits, Terry transferred to the railroad ferry *The Santa Maria*. The Coast Guard ice breaker cleared a channel in the Straits for the railroad ferry: it alone could withstand the chunks of ice floating in the channel—the other ferries were laid up for the winter.

I drove up to the Straits one Sunday to ride the ferry on the last trip across on Terry's shift. He came out to meet me.

"I think I'll stand out here in front of the pilot house: I'd like to watch the ferry maneuver in this small channel."

"Okay, but it'll be a cold trip."

As we got underway, the wheelsman turned the ferry into the edge of the solid field of ice. It sounded like a rifle shot as the ice split from the main field. I jumped at the sound: that brought smiles to the faces of the men inside the pilot house. I learned later that they keep breaking into the main field of ice to keep the channel open. It *was* cold standing out on deck but I enjoyed every bit of it. (I wore Terry's hair seal hat with the flaps over my ears on this trip.) Northern Michigan is an enchanting place in the winter with Terry around.

One evening, he was more quiet than usual and I wondered why. Finally he said: "I am nineteen years old; I'll be twenty in February. I don't want my mother to sign for me on a marriage license: we'd need to wait another year to be married.

"Is this a proposal? If so, what's the problem?"

"You'll wait for me then." He looked so relieved. He knew I was older than he too—he thought women didn't like to marry men who were younger.

I kissed him good-night and knew this was the man I would be with the rest of my life.

Christmas Eve of that year, Terry gave me our engagement ring. On June 14, 1950, we were married at St. Francis Xavier Church with a Solemn High Mass offered by the priests whom we had known so long: Father Hugolinus,

Father Benign and Father Venard. The choir sang the various parts of the Mass which included the Gloria and Credo because it occurred during the octave of Corpus Christi.

Mom and Dad were there—my sister Georgia, my brother Richard, my best friend Elizabeth, Terry's sister Virginia and her husband Gene were in the wedding party. The women of the Altar Society of the parish prepared and served the breakfast. As we drove through town later, all the flags were flying—no, not for us: June 14 is Flag Day.

Our first home was a tiny third-floor apartment of a beautiful old large house across the street from Bear Creek. We could hear the water flow over the dam on its way to Little Traverse Bay. From the window in the living room, we watched the sun set in the middle of the Bay. Petoskey was known as the City of the Million Dollar Sunsets.

We started our married life saying our evening prayer together; even when apart, we knew the other was saying the same evening prayer. Early on, we felt a need for some more spiritual direction. This led us to a lay religious order, The Third Order of St. Francis. (We're now known as the Secular Franciscan Order.) It made us part of a worldwide spiritual family. The priests comprise the First Order, the Poor Clare cloistered nuns, the Second Order.

Twelve children were born to us, each one such a treasure. Two of them died a few hours after birth: we have them as our special intercessors in heaven. Our days were filled with joys and sorrows, ups and downs: having a good sense of humor helped a lot. Mother Mary Francis, P.C.C., a Poor Clare nun, said in her book, *A Right to be Merry,* that a real sense of humor balances the mysteries of joys and sorrows.

Terry always urged me on to newer things when I tended to become too content with caring for the children. That brought us to live in Costa Rica for two years. I wrote about that in a book, titled *Ten Ambassadors to Costa Rica.*

Chapter III

Let's Go for It

We enjoyed our work in Costa Rica; there was a slight counter-culture shock when we settled in Ft. Worth, Texas, upon our return. We lived in a hotel in downtown Ft. Worth until we found a house to rent. The younger children were amazed at the large stores where you could buy anything and everything—they didn't even close for a couple of hours at midday. Our youngest son, Hilary, four years old at the time, was looking at the display in the meat market one day where we were shopping.

"Are all the chickens here dead?"

"No, but that's all you'll see around here in the city—I know it's a lot different from Nicoya: All the neighbors had live ones running around in their yards there."

Not too many people were willing to rent a house to a family with ten children. We checked out all the ads in the paper every day. Eventually, we found one—a beautiful old, two-story house with an open staircase and fireplaces. The family who owned it moved to a more residential area—this house was surrounded by commercial buildings now. It suited our needs though at the present time. Near the downtown area, most everything, including the cathedral, was in reach with short bus rides—Terry needed our car as he searched for employment.

The house had a stove, refrigerator and dining room furniture. Our shipment from Costa Rica contained dishes, utensils and bed clothes along with the desk and files; the latter were needed for making out the second annual report for USAID, beds could come later: We were in business.

A few weeks later, Brigid, at the age of five, became quite ill: her skin had a yellowish tint. Terry had looked like this in Michigan years ago when he contracted hepatitis drinking water from a contaminated well where he worked.

I found a pediatrician in the phone book whose office was near.

"My daughter Brigid has symptoms of hepatitis; can you help us?"

"Are you qualified to diagnose an illness?"

"Doctor, my husband had it years ago and I remember how he looked; I just didn't want us to come and sit in your waiting room with the other children there."

"You let me be the judge of that when you get here."

Terry Jr. and I took a taxi to the office. (Terry had the car that morning.) In the waiting room, we sat in a corner away from the other children until our name was called. The doctor examined Brigid.

"Look how swollen her liver is—she has hepatitis. Do you realize you've been sitting out there with those other children?"

"I told you that when I phoned you but you didn't listen to me."

"Take her to the hospital immediately: go through this back door."

Terry carried her to the nearby hospital. We checked her in at the admittance office; she was put into an isolation room—a very sick little girl.

Terry Jr. returned home to the other children: I didn't worry about them. At lunchtime, the nurse brought in food for Brigid: a chicken pot pie. I remembered that was not the type of food on the list the doctor gave me when Terry had hepatitis.

"Would you please take this tray back and bring her food with a lot of sugar in it or just plain protein and no fat."

"I'll take it back and tell them what you said."

She returned with another tray. A short time later, the doctor came in.

"What gives you the authority to tell the kitchen what Brigid should or should not have: we know what she needs."

"Then, why did they bring what I asked for if it was not good for her?"

Needless to say, we did not have a good doctor-patient relationship.

I felt completely lost and desperate. As I looked at Brigid and saw the color of her skin, the yellowness in her eyes, near panic set in.

Then I saw a man come in the glassed-in area by the door where everyone gowned before coming into the room. He nodded to me as he entered and went over to the bed and looked at Brigid.

"Hi, Brigid. I'm a priest from a neighboring parish and I bring Holy Communion to Catholic patients. I was leaving the hospital just now and decided to take another look at the book to see if anyone was admitted after I came in. There I saw Brigid McCarthy's name and that she was Catholic so here I am. But you look a little too young to have prepared to receive Communion so here is Jesus in the host: He blesses you and will make you well."

All my fear left and complete calm returned—I knew she'd get well. During the night, when I helped her go to the bathroom, her urine, which had been the color of Coca Cola, now had streaks of clear water also. Ultimately, she was released from the hospital a day and a half later, all signs of hepatitis gone.

We started registering the children in school: I had quite a packet containing all the required papers for each child. Terry Jr., Kevin, and Rory were enrolled in middle school; Bob, Cronan, Sean, Christopher and Brigid in grade school. The certificates we had from the Calvert Correspondence School were accepted and all of them progressed to the next grade level. (We used Calvert Correspondence Courses in Costa Rica.) They walked to school together in the morning—kindergarten class, however, ended at noon: Hilary, Camille and I met Brigid every day when her class ended.

One afternoon, the four of us were sitting on the front steps of the house waiting for the older boys to come home from school. The house was near the railroad tracks; a man from that vicinity walked up the sidewalk toward us. He sat on the grass near us, talking with us—Hilary told him we were waiting for the older boys to come home from school; then the man started looking at the open front door of the house. I felt very uneasy—what was the best thing to do: go into the house or stay where we were. Just then I caught sight of all the boys coming down the sidewalk—what a great sight that was. The man left immediately.

Terry had a temporary job but kept looking for other employment. One day, he remembered an article he read years before in a magazine, *The Co-operator,* published by the R. G. LeTourneau Company—they manufactured heavy equipment. He had the magazine in his file and reread the article: A Heavy Equipment Training Center opened at the Texas A&M Engineering Extension Center in College Station, Texas.

He wrote to Alvin Jones at the center—he received an answer from him requesting an interview. Terry went to College Station and was hired. I had the car now: that helped with the task of removing the children from school and the usual moving jobs. Terry came home on the bus on weekends until he found housing for the family in Bryan, Texas, a short distance from College Station.

The house he found was adequate but as winter approached, we had difficulty keeping warm—there was no basement: the open space below the house left the floors icy cold. Space heaters didn't help that situation. The wind blew across the open prairie—I never knew Texas could be that cold: quite a difference after living in the tropics.

Terry Jr. and Kevin transferred to junior high at the public school in Bryan. They walked to school; there was a Catholic church on the way—they took their breakfast with them and served Mass every day. Rory, Bob, Cronan, Sean, Christopher and Brigid went to St. Joseph's Catholic School.

Coming back to the Catholic Church in the States in 1967 provided another shock. When Terry volunteered to teach CCD classes, he met with a lot of confusion—some were doing their own interpretation of the Second Vatican Council Documents regarding doctrine.

The pastor of the church where Terry and Kevin served Mass every day came to the house quite often—we didn't always agree with what he had to say.

"In dealing with marriage problems, I can't tell the couple they should stay together when they're just not compatible."

"Father, I'm glad you didn't counsel us—by dealing with differences, we matured physically and spiritually."

"But things are different in the Church now."

"Father, things like that don't change."

We had lively discussions but he kept coming back for more.

The priest at the Newman Center at College Station also had his own interpretations. One was having everyone gather alongside him by the altar during the Consecration of the Mass: more lively discussions followed.

The bulletin in our parish church had an article announcing a retreat available in Houston—Terry felt he needed to attend it. The retreat itself didn't help too much; however, he purchased a paperback copy of the *Documents of Vatican II* while there. We studied them and focused on "The Church in the Modern World" and "The Role of the Laity" in the Documents; we didn't see any changes in the doctrine: We managed to steer clear of the misinterpretations that way.

Terry trained men in operating and maintaining heavy equipment at the Texas A&M Engineering Extension Service field operation: a six-week course. One of the men who took the course was an artist. He suffered from emotional problems at the time: his wife was killed in an auto accident. The doctor recommended doing something entirely different from his art work to help him during this time. Terry learned a completely new way of training working with Frank DeCardenas: his delicate hands moved the levers on the machines with a dramatic flourish. He proved to be a very good student.

Terry occasionally invited him to dinner; he was fascinated by all our children at the table: he called them our Midgets. Frank always brought along an exquisitely shaped bottle of wine of some sort when he came to dinner. One time, he brought a gin-soaked watermelon for dessert—the gin was injected into the watermelon with a hypodermic needle; he brought a plain one for the Midgets.

He enjoyed the home cooking and wanted to paint something for me—I requested a picture of Jesus, His eyes showing the deep love He has for us. Frank came to the house one afternoon with a picture; a cloth covered the front—he told me to turn around as he placed the picture on the chair.

"Turn around now."

I turned and looked at the picture. He stood there watching my face—then picked up the picture and started to leave.

"Frank, where are you going with it?"

"I watched your face and knew it was not what you wanted—I'm taking it back."

He was gone before I could say anything else.

Another student, Art Leon, worked in Central America for a time; he was on his way to Alaska to work and decided to take the heavy equipment training in College Station before going to Alaska. He also came to dinner quite often. I received a Mothers' Day card from him later in the year from Alaska— *"again thanks, to you and your fine family, for everything. Art Leon."*

That first summer in Bryan, Terry Jr. and Kevin baled hay for a rancher; one afternoon I heard a knock on the front door. There stood Kevin and the rancher.

"Mrs. McCarthy, Kevin was knocked off the top of the load of hay by a branch of a tree. He was unconscious for a while and then I took him to our doctor: he said he was okay."

"Thank you."

Kevin still looked very pale so I took him to the emergency room to make sure it wasn't a concussion. He checked out okay but his whole body ached horribly: he spent many miserable days and nights.

Rory and Bob cut the neighbors' lawns that summer—our Sears mower didn't work out too well. When they mowed lawns in the neighborhood, I dreaded hearing a loud thud and then silence: what broke this time! The Sears repairman got to know them quite well.

"I know you boys are using this mower only for your own lawn—I hope you find all the hidden obstacles soon."

We finally found it necessary to purchase another mower—we tried one from Penney's: the Briggs and Stratton motor on that one worked a lot better.

The boys also learned that summer what chigger bites were—they picked blackberries.

"Mom, the pies are well worth the discomfort," is what we usually heard at the dinner table.

The Engineering Extension Service had a large area of open ground where the heavy equipment training was done. On weekends, Terry Jr., Kevin, Rory and Bob often spent time there. One particular Sunday, Bob's school friend, David Becka, was with them as they explored a small stream. David walked downstream in about six inches of water—suddenly he began sinking in the sandy bottom: his feet disappeared. He tried to free himself but only sank deeper. Bob ran to help him.

"David, don't try to get out—we'll find a way to get you out."

"Okay, but please hurry—I'm scared."

"I think we can dig you out but we'll have to do it with our hands: there's nothing else here."

The first attempts proved futile as the water replenished the sand. David's knees vanished but then the sinking stabilized. The four boys began digging dog style at one leg and finally managed to extricate it. Bob held on to that leg while the other boys dug the other one out. Who would've thought they'd find quicksand in Texas.

David went to St. Joseph's School with Bob so we often saw his family at church and at school functions. His mother called me one day.

"Thecla, I know of a house that you can rent that is much closer to College Station than where you live now. We would take it but my husband has decided to take the offer he received from a university in the state of Washington as professor of philosophy. I'll take you to see the house if you wish."

"I'll be right over."

I blessed the day she told me about it—she was the mother of eight children and she knew it would be perfect for our family.

The house was a large older one with special rooms I loved. The entryway led to an open stairway and the bedrooms upstairs—to the left, a door opened to the large living room with a hardwood floor and a beautiful fireplace, to the right was a small wood-paneled office. In the back part of the house, the original owner, an artist, designed one of the rooms with floor-to-ceiling windows for the desired lighting to do his art work. The combined kitchen and dining room occupied the entire width of the house on one side, overlooking a small city stream. The front paneled window of the dining room framed a young maple tree in the front yard.

Terry and the older boys put many hours of work into the house before we moved there. At one time, it housed a pre-school—there was evidence of rooms used for classrooms: letters of the alphabet lined some of the walls. College students occupied it after that—we took over after they left at the end of the semester. Kevin's truck hauled away the loads of paper and discarded items that the boys gathered from all the rooms. The beautiful hardwood floors were sanded and varnished with loving care.

The house stood only a few blocks from the main highway linking Bryan and College Station but resembled a country setting with the large front lawn shaded by a huge live oak tree and the young maple tree by the front window; the little stream alongside the house supported more large trees: quiet and peaceful.

Once, when the spring rain flooded the little stream alongside the house, a mother opossum brought her little ones on the back porch for safety; we had fun feeding them during her stay.

It would be hard to leave all of this, but going to Suriname to live sounded fascinating. One evening in June of 1969, Terry and I were having a cup of coffee at the kitchen table.

"Terry, I think you should call Mr. Brenn and tell him we accept the offer."

"Okay, let's go for it."

During the weeks that followed, we read all the information Alcoa sent us about Suriname—it is the former Dutch Guyana, located on the northeast coast of South America. In 1667, the British gave up Guyana for what is now New York while the Dutch gave up New York for Guyana—a real swinging swap. At this time, Suriname is a part of the Netherlands empire, which consists of Holland, Suriname and the islands of the Greater Antilles. Suriname is often called the UN in miniature. The people and their well-preserved cultures make up a tapestry of togetherness.

The northern coastline consists of a muddy beach—the mud is transported by the Amazon River to the Atlantic Ocean and deposited along the coast by a westerly Gulf Stream: how unlike the white sand beaches we saw in Costa Rica.

A new bauxite mine was scheduled to open on August 29, 1969. Lelydorp would provide the raw material for the production of alumina, aluminum and dried and calcined bauxites for export. The ore is buried fifty to one hundred feet deep: the 1350-W dragline, largest of its kind on the South American continent, would remove the thick layer of overburden. Terry was scheduled to assume the duties there of Training Supervisor of Shop and Field—a new position established in the Engineering Department of Suralco.

Regarding our family, Alcoa agreed to provide high school correspondence courses from the University of Nebraska for the boys in high school—we were familiar with that type of education. All systems were "go": we were ready to try living in South America. I looked forward to seeing new cultures in Suriname: Dutch, Hindu, Creole, Bush Negro and Javanese.

In the packet we received from Alcoa were the forms for complete physicals for the whole family. Terry knew he had a double hernia: Texas A & M gave him a waiver on it when he started work there. Alcoa insisted upon the operation on the hernia for employment with them—that was taken care of at the local hospital. It took much scheduling of appointments for the rest of the family but all went well.

Alcoa furnished the houses for the expatriates in Suriname so a minimum of items for the household was needed: the rest we owned needed to be sold—not a favorite job of mine but we accomplished it.

We bought a duffel bag for each of the children and shopped for the types of clothing suggested by the company: Suriname is near the equator so light summer clothes and swim suits were in order.

Times when I felt overwhelmed by all of these tasks, I went to the little stream by the house and sat in the shade of the trees on the bank to watch it in its travels—soon our travels would take us to another part of the world.

REFLECTIONS

City stream, fighting daily
to clear dirt from your face
and reveal your many charms.
Today you do look beautiful;
your quiet pool upstream
reflects branches, streaks of sunlight.

But lovely green leaf
why do you come twirling down?
Does the gleam of your reflection
bid you on?

June bewitches and uses
her colors to lure you on
where the choreographers,
water and breeze,
display your talents,
Tempo adagio.

But now the swifter water
picks up the beat—you're caught
swirling, whirling—ecstatic
until you pause—
in a little harbor—
gracefully wedged ever so tightly
among brown, dead leaves.
They too left their source of life
to dance, dream, laugh one day.

Today my edges are worn thin,
tasks seem unending,
but please, little leaf,
take what comfort lies
in knowing that I learned
a lesson well today.

WHAT A DAD

From the yard I hear the doorbell ring
"Mommy, there's someone here."
I drop the wet jeans and hurry in
there stand the kids, wearing big grins.

One holds a box, long and thin
Wrapped in folds of green ribbon
with sprigs of fern peeking through and
tiny velvet birds perched upon
a swirl of downy netting.

The card bearing
the words you tenderly wrote
bring tears; my heart overflows—
"Why do you cry, Mommy?"

Luscious luxury and sheer delight
there in the box lie
long-stemmed roses of white.

How it amazes the children
that Dad could send them when
high in the sky he's been
since morning, when they prayed:
"May he journey safely today."

My lips touch each lovely rose,
caress each soft, velvety petal
so like the skin of the newborn babes
I nestled in years gone by.

Thank you, my husband,
what a precious way to make you feel near
until we're together again.

Chapter IV

Krakalaan 13

Terry arrived in Suriname July 3, 1969, just in time for the celebration of America's Independence Day. He assumed his duties as mobile equipment training director at the Paranam Operations. At home, the same day, I received the box of white long-stemmed roses—how I loved this man, the father of my children.

He was living in a motel the company maintained in Paranam: a village near the mine. However, he decided to retain it even after we arrived—the manager of mine production at Paranam transferred to another mine in Moengo, a village near the border with French Guyana. Terry was asked to take over that position on an interim basis before resuming the training duties. As production manager, he needed to be at the mine site at all hours of the day and night.

Back home in the USA, Terry Jr. and Kevin were traveling with a wheat harvest crew through the Midwest—they started in Texas shortly after school was out for the summer; they hoped to be in the Dakotas in August and join us in Suriname at the end of August. The high school courses were ordered from the University of Nebraska Correspondence School; they were scheduled to arrive in Suriname about the time the boys did.

Rory, Bob, Cronan, Sean, Chris, Brigid, Hilary, Camille and I were finishing the packing and the last minute closing of the house. Our friends Ed and Marge Patke and family had a farewell dinner for us—Marge's fried chicken was beyond compare—the empty platters were evidence of it.

On Sunday, July 20, 1969, Chris's teacher, whose name also was Armstrong, appeared at our front door with a TV.

"I know you don't have a TV anymore and you're busy with all the last minute responsibilities and haven't had time to think about other things; I don't want the children to miss this great moment in history when man lands on the moon tonight."

"Thank you so much, Mrs. Armstrong—that is so thoughtful of you. You're a wonderful teacher."

We set the TV on the floor in the living room; later that evening, we all sat on the floor (all the furniture was gone) and watched Neil Armstrong step onto the moon at precisely 10:56 p.m. What a memorable day! When Terry called us later, he said: "The local people stopped me on the street, shook my hand and congratulated me because an American landed on the moon."

Alcoa Steamship allowed passengers aboard their cargo ships—I requested passage for the children and me on one that was sailing to Suriname shortly. My request was denied—I was told it was too dangerous with that many small children on board.

Now our duffel bags were filling up; I was concerned about the weight limit required on our plane ticket. Rory, who was working at his friend's outdoor produce market, brought home a produce scale. I hung it on the door in the kitchen and suspended each duffel bag on the hook of the scale. All the bags were at or below the limit. He also brought home wonderful fruits which were getting too old to keep another day—to us they were at the peak of their goodness and were thoroughly enjoyed.

The last day we moved to a motel. The following morning, July 30, 1969, we took a taxi to the Bryan/College Station Airport. It hit me, as we prepared to board Trans Texas Airline (sometimes referred to as Tree Top Airline), that no one was there to see us off—just the city of Bryan to say good-bye to as we left to live in another country.

Our first stop was Houston; there, the children rode the little tram cars connecting the different gates: an enjoyable way to pass the time between flights and meet lots of people. Our next destination: Miami.

We spent the rest of the day in the hotel at the airport in Miami. That evening, Cronan was leading the children into the dining room for dinner. The maitre d' grabbed the back of the collar of his shirt and began pulling him back.

"Please let go of my son."

"I'm sorry, ma'am, I didn't see you—I thought the children were alone."

"That still was no reason for you to grab him in that fashion."

"I'm sorry. May I seat you, please"

He led us to a large round table that accommodated all of us. As we finished dinner, a gentleman sitting at a nearby table came over to us.

"I wanted to let you know how much my wife and I enjoyed seeing all of you here—the children's table manners were exemplary."

"Thank you, sir."

The next morning we were off to Suriname. Now we would see the Caribbean Islands—when we went to Costa Rica, we visited cities in Central America.

Our first stop out of Miami was Kingston, Jamaica—how different it was from those we made on our way through Central America. No soft, lyrical sounds of the Spanish language were heard—here the Jamaican English had a distinct sound. The musical group greeting us inside the terminal introduced us to their type of rhythm and musical sounds—all in all, a very different feeling. I thought about the descriptions of Kingston in the book *The White Witch of Rosehall*. Yes, the scenery is beautiful but there is also the sinister feeling of the people's belief in obeah that I read about in the book.

Our next stop was the Dutch island of Curacao—now the sound of the Dutch language introduced us to the main language we would hear in Suriname: a harsh, guttural sound. Even though many spoke Dutch, the local language was called Papimento: a combination of Dutch, Spanish and English.

It was dark when we started the last stretch of our flight from Curacao to Georgetown, Guyana, and then on to Suriname. KLM was noted for the excellent and continuous serving of food on their flights. The children's tummies were full and they were now sound asleep.

I looked out the window at the complete darkness of the water below: no ships, no lights of any kind—just dark, dark water—a very lonely feeling.

I started thinking about the heroine of my younger years—Amelia Earhart. In 1937, she attempted to become the first person to circumnavigate the world at its widest point, the equator. She and her navigator, Fred Noonan, must have had some really lonely feelings too flying across large stretches of water before they disappeared over the Pacific and were never seen again. That also brought back memories of my determination to take a ride in an open-cockpit plane. Would I accomplish this in Suriname?

Finally, far off in the distance, I saw the flash of an airport beacon. No other lights were visible anywhere as we approached the northern shore of South America.

After a short stop in Georgetown, Guyana (British Guyana), we flew east along the coast until the lights of Paramaribo and Zanderij Airport greeted us. We were in Suriname.

Dad was waiting for us—it was so good to see him: we were a family again. With a VW van to accommodate the family and the luggage, we started the rather lengthy trip on the left side of the two-lane highway to the capitol city of Paramaribo.

Our new home was located at Krakalaan 13, Via Bella—Alcoa built homes in this section of the city for the Americans working for the Suriname Aluminum Company (Suralco).

The living room lights were on—a vase of fresh flowers on the coffee table, seen through the sliding glass doors, welcomed us. Mrs. Beachem, wife of the manager of the engineering department, thought of everything to make us feel at home. Fresh towels on the turned-down beds awaited the arrival of a family of very tired and late-night travelers: how grateful we were!

Early the next morning after breakfast, Terry and I toured the rest of the house and surroundings. It was a ranch-style house typical of those in the States—quite different from our house in Costa Rica: a plain, square wooden one.

The large sliding-glass door opened from the carport into the living room; a decorative room divider separated that room from the dining room. A corner of the dining room afforded space for our desk; another part was open to a sitting room with a sliding glass door to the backyard; to the right a door led into the kitchen. The other half of the house contained the four bedrooms and two baths.

The kitchen was very small, just enough room for the stove, refrigerator, sink and limited counter space and cabinets: all meals were eaten in the dining room. Two tables pushed together were needed to accommodate the family— that took up quite a bit of room. (Later, since there were no tablecloths large enough to cover them to make them look like one table, I bought enough material at the department store to cover both tables: solved that problem.)

The front yard was home to a huge rubber tree while the backyard had two tropical pine trees with their grey-green needles and a huge mango tree. There were also ample clotheslines on one end of the yard. Most everyone here still hung their clothes outside unlike most housing associations in the States that forbid that now.

Then Terry was off to work: he drove to Paranam about twenty-five kilometers south of Paramaribo—the mine, the smelter and the docks, known as the Paranam Works, were located there. The highway was completed just a few months before his arrival—formerly, there were only indirect roads which made the travel time an hour and a half each way.

Later in the morning, I walked into the kitchen to start breakfast for the children—there was the face of a pretty young lady smiling at me through the window. She was sitting on her bike in the part of the carport by our kitchen window.

"Hi, I'm Jackie Rose, your neighbor from across the street—I'm anxious to meet all of you; I've never known a family with that many children."

"Hi, Jackie. There are eight of them here now and two more coming at the end of August. I'm afraid the eight here are still a little groggy this morning. I'm sure they'll be happy to meet you a little later."

"We live in that corner house across the street," she continued. "Your neighbor on this side of your house is a Dutch family—the father is in charge of the electric power company in Paramaribo; your neighbor on the other side is Hindustani—I don't know what he does; your neighbor behind is also Dutch but he works for Suralco."

"Thanks for all the information, Jackie; I'm sure we'll get to know them in time."

"Hear that funny-sounding motor—that's the milkman coming. There he is in that little three-wheeled cart going by: he steers the cart with that metal post in front of him. You can hear him long before he gets here."

"I'm sure we'll find things a lot different here but that's okay."

"Oh, you'll have to learn to drive on the left side of the street too—that was really hard for my mom."

"I'm sure that'll take a lot of time for me to master too—Jackie, would you like to park your bike and come in?"

"No, I'll come later when all the kids are awake—bye now."

"Thanks for stopping by, Jackie."

She was a delightful young lady and remained friends with our family long after our return to the States.

And so our new way of life began. Our first adventure developed a couple of days after our arrival—Rory had a bad toothache. Where to look for a dentist? The American neighbors didn't know of one. We got on a city bus at the entrance to Villa Bella hoping to ultimately find a bus that would take us to the Suralco office. We arrived at a bus center in the downtown area. A young girl, who had a boyfriend from British Guyana, spoke English and helped us find the bus for the transfer.

I talked with the company doctor at the Suralco office. He had his driver take us to a dentist in his car. The dentist spoke some English.

"I never thought someone coming from the States would have need of a dentist so soon after his arrival."

I think he was trying to tell me we were lax in the proper care of the children's teeth. Be that as it may, he took care of Rory's tooth; we found our way back home on the bus—we felt pretty satisfied with our accomplishment.

In the information that Alcoa sent us before we came, we learned it was customary for families to hire a maid—that is how Jane Holder was added to the family. When Jane came to apply, she looked at the size of the family.

"I'll try it for two weeks and let you know what I decide."

She was with us until we left—when we later moved to Paranam, she rode the bus there every day. She was Creole; on special occasions she wore an anjisa (a starched bandana-type headdress folded in a certain way to indicate her status in society). She lived in Paramaribo near the Suriname River and rode the bus to Via Bella every day. She spoke Dutch and Takie-Takie (a combination of Dutch, Javanese and several other languages); she soon picked up some English words talking with the children. Bob teased her a lot.

"Mommy, Mommy, Bob bad boy," was heard frequently as she came looking for me.

When we attempted to take her picture a few weeks after she arrived, she panicked and tried to hide.

"What's the matter, Jane—it won't hurt you."

"No, no." Her eyes were wide with terror.

Jane thought that her spirit would come out of her into the picture. As time went on, she saw the many pictures we took of our family and friends with no ill effect. We were surprised and happy when she came to the house on her "day off" celebrating a Creole holiday. She wanted her picture taken with her children: Jane and her daughters were wearing their *anjisas*.

Thecla with Jane and her daughters (wearing their *anjisas*) and son.

Shortly after we arrived in Suriname, I read an article in the company newsletter: Paramaribo, Suriname—Oil companies bought a large tract of land bordering the city of Paramaribo from the government of Suriname. This was to be used for a tank farm for storing gas.

This bit of news in the local newsletter didn't seem very unusual unless you knew that the government had purchased the land from the Catholic Church. The Church no longer had use of it because the population there had dwindled to nothing. Instead of this being a disheartening development, it was on the contrary, a joyous occasion because this had been a leper colony. Modern medicine had halted the ravages of the disease and there was no longer any need for the land.

But the marks of the disease can still be seen any day on the streets of Paramaribo—a lady without a nose, only two holes, another with deep scars on the legs, a man with a crippled leg, another without fingers, still others with club feet because the toes were gone—all ex-Hansen patients.

Our neighbor, Mrs. Lohan, a Dutch lady, invited me to come with her to the rehabilitation center for these ex-Hansen patients. She volunteered there several days a week and wanted me to see the articles for sale there—I accepted.

The center was downtown on Tourtennelaan—a small building: one part was a store, another part stored the materials used by the patients; an adjoining screened-in area held tables and chairs where the actual work was done.

A group of women organized to work with these ex-Hansen patients to buy materials, help prepare these materials for the work to be done and package them for selling. The patients themselves did all the handiwork—they received payment for their work; the women helping them volunteered their time. I volunteered there two days a week after that visit.

The patients still lived together in the city as they did in the leper colony outside the city years ago. They still were not accepted for domestic work—people did not like them working in their homes. Here at the center, the women did beautiful embroidery and lace work; the men fashioned the jewelry. Some of the work was done at home if the patient wasn't able to get to the center.

It was such a joy to be around them. They were a happy group despite their handicaps. One lady I saw embroidering a design in a napkin, held the needle with her middle knuckles—all that was left of her fingers. The women did beautiful work: tablecloths, napkins, handkerchiefs, tea cozies.

I didn't know what a tea cozy was until I saw them working on them. The finished product looked like a beautifully-dressed rag doll standing on the table. Inspecting the doll revealed the base was thick and firm—it would fit over the tea pot to keep the tea warm until the second cup was served. The doll was dressed as a Koto-Missie doll—the ample material of the dress top and skirt covered the thick base. Koto-Missie was the name given to feminine slaves in the early days of the country—the full top and skirt of the dress and the anijsa headdress was mandatory to disguise the shape of the women while they worked among the plantation owners.

The embroidery designs on all the articles depicted people of the five distinct cultures: Dutch, Hindus, Javanese, Creoles and Bush Negroes in their ethnic clothes—just as they were seen by us every day. The men designed jewelry and did beautiful wood carvings. Koebie stones were often used in the jewelry—beautiful white stones found in the head of the koebie fish, a delicious fresh-water fish.

The volunteers purchased all the materials used—they bought the linen and cotton material and prepared it for the articles needed. I watched them at first as they pulled threads to insure straight cuts of the material. That definitely was not my line of expertise. I turned to the packaging of the finished articles; this was also done by hand—handkerchiefs were folded and attached to construction paper with needle and thread and wrapped in plastic; the jewelry also was packaged in the same manner; tablecloths and napkins were wrapped in plastic. The items were sold in the store at the center and also at hotels and stores in the city.

Going to the center also gave me the one chance to see something quite unusual. One morning a large group of people gathered in the street in front of the center. Paramaribo is at sea level: deep drainage ditches along the streets necessitated small wooden walkways across the ditches to give access to the buildings. There in the ditch that morning lay the largest in diameter snake I had I had ever seen in my life: a carpet snake. The colorful pattern on the skin resembled the design of the old-fashioned carpet. The people standing around were watching several men picking up the snake to place it into the bed of a truck—it appeared to be quite docile. I noticed they talked in whispers while they worked. I learned later they believe the carpet snake can hear and understand what they say: they want to make sure they don't say anything to offend them in any way.

The center became an important part of our life and is woven throughout our story.

Our house soon was the hub of most of the activities of the children in the neighborhood—some Americans, some local children of Dutch descent, some Hindustani, others of Creole and Javanese descent. Sometimes those activities included me. Bob came in the kitchen one day.

"Mom, I heard you tell Dad you'll be learning to drive the VW bus on the streets here in Via Bella before you tackle the streets in the city. With the steering wheel on the right side of the bus, you'll be using the stick shift with your left hand when driving on the left side of the street: you'll need to practice lot."

"Yes, there's hardly any traffic here during the day—I plan to do a lot of stopping and starting to learn to shift."

Cronan joined in the conversation.

"We got this neat idea, Mom. Some of us will pretend we're Marines, some will be the enemy; we can pretend the bus is a helicopter—when you stop, we'll slide the side door open and jump out to fight the enemy."

"If you take the same route every day," added Bob, "back where there are no houses right now, we can plan our strategy."

I saw no harm in trying the plan—ultimately, I learned to drive doing the many starts and stops needed to master shifting with my left hand; meanwhile, the troops jumped out and were picked up at designated areas: many battles were fought and won during that time.

A Green Beret slide was added in the pine trees in the backyard. Cronan earned some money house-sitting for Americans while they were on vacation. With some of the money, he bought a length of half-inch rope.

"Rory, let's make a slide like we saw the Green Beret use at that 4th of July celebration when we lived in Ft. Worth."

"Yeah, that was great to see them slide from the top of one big building to the bottom of another building across the street."

"That pine tree is high enough to attach one end of the rope," added Bob.

"Okay, I think that fence post across the yard will serve as an anchor."

"I brought those carabiners from Bryan, Texas—remember, we found them on the ground when we spent weekends exploring the heavy equipment training grounds at Texas A & M."

"They should be the right size. We can use that ammunition belt as a sling to sit on."

Up the tree Cronan climbed and attached the rope—Rory anchored the other end to the fence post. I heard a squeal of delight and there came Cronan sliding down the rope, laughing all the way. He landed to the applause of all the kids.

Another thing they delved into was building a human pyramid: Bob was attempting to complete the third level of the pyramid and fell in the process, breaking his arm: we could see the bone. (That was the only broken bone ever suffered in our family.) That necessitated our first visit to a doctor—the Suralco office gave us directions to the clinic. It was in the vicinity of our house and not too risky for my driving expertise.

We sat on a bench outside the building waiting for our turn. When our name was called, the doctor looked at Bob's arm—he sent us across the courtyard to a building where the x-rays were done. They called Bob's name and we went to the door indicated; I opened the door and three people, wearing the usual white jackets seen in clinics, were having a great time inside; one was sitting on the patient's table, dramatically relating some incident to another person: the third person approached me.

"You don't need to come in with him, ma'am; we'll take care of him."

"What are you going to do for him?"

"We'll give him a shot and then x-ray his arm."

I saw no need for a shot just to x-ray his arm and asked what kind of shot this would be. They didn't want to share that information with me.

"I'm going to stay here with him."

That was not tolerable to them so Bob and I were soon on our way home to seek other options. Ultimately, Terry was able to contact some people after he came home and Bob's arm was x-rayed and put in a cast that evening. Finding a good family doctor is always on top of the list when traveling with a family—here it was proving to be quite difficult.

I contracted some kind of tropical fever which kept me bedridden for a time—Jane tried to convince me to take some "over-the-counter" syrup to cure it. The label on the bottle she brought to me boasted of its ability to cure anything and everything and the caricature depicted on the label left nothing to the imagination. I thanked her for bringing it but declined keeping it or taking any of it.

The next day, Jane came into the bedroom shortly after she arrived at the house; I was lying on my side with my back to her. She called out to me and as I rolled over to answer her, she stuck a spoon into my mouth—the syrup was down before I realized what happened—she quickly left the room. I don't know whether my body was already healing itself of the fever or whether my reaction to the taste of the syrup drove it out, but I was definitely on the mend after that.

As I continued to recover, I spent some of the time on the couch in the sitting room by the dining room. The neighborhood kids congregated there with ours when the midday heat was too much for them—they kept me company. The number kept growing—the three Lohan girls who were our Dutch neighbors, Jackie, Mark and Tracey Rose, Jane Sharkey, Jack and Mary Nevins, and the Fitzgibbon children, all Alcoa expatriates, and later, Steve Serdahely Jr. joined us: his dad worked for World Health.

As I regained my energy, I sat on the back patio—such beautiful views from a most common backyard: the children playing, the freshly washed sheets billowing high into the air as the breeze swished through the long, flowing needles of the pine tree. It was a sweet melancholy sound reminiscent of those heard years ago at Cross Village on Lake Michigan—those pine trees were robust and bright green color while these in the tropics look fragile and wispy and gray-green in color.

In the evening, the haughty, elegant palm trees in the neighbor's yard were silhouetted against the last golden rays of the sun on the clouds. Each palm sported its new antenna, reaching tall and thin from the center: they will gracefully bend and join their sister fronds in a few days, their soft shade of green the only evidence of their recent birth.

At the end of August, Terry Jr. and Kevin arrived from the States. About the same time, notice came to us through the Suralco office that the high school correspondence courses had arrived from the University of Nebraska: the shipment could be picked up at the post office downtown.

Driving on the left side of the street in the city was now tolerable; armed with a city map and the notice from Suralco, Rory and I headed downtown to the post office. There, each window had a long line of customers waiting; we picked the one we thought looked the most likely to have what we needed and waited. I approached the window and handed the man my notice. He looked it over put his initials on it and handed it back.

"Go over to *that* window to pick it up."

"Thank you."

My heart fell when I saw the line at that window. Oh well, it'll soon be over and we'll be on our way. When I approached this window, the man was very gracious.

"We'll bring out the boxes and help you load them in your car. But there is also another package for you—it's a small one and is at *that* window over there."

I tried to smile as I thanked him; we finally picked up that package—it was from Frank DeCardenas, the artist that Terry trained to operate heavy equipment at Texas A&M months before. The note read: "I tried calling you to visit you and give you this painting but you were gone—the University gave me your address. I couldn't paint the picture you wanted so I painted this one for the Midgets." (It was a picture of a teddy bear—very different from any other teddy bear we'd ever seen: a little grotesque but perhaps we didn't appreciate some of the modern art.)

We obtained some desks from Suralco to accommodate the boys doing the high school courses—one was in the hall, the others in part of the bedrooms. The literature accompanying the courses indicated the university preferred someone from the consulate conducting the tests to be taken.

When I called the wife of the consulate, she graciously accepted the task. Terry Jr. in twelfth grade; Kevin, tenth grade; and Rory, ninth grade, went to meet her.

"I'll look forward to giving the tests to you as you finish the work. Now let me hear what you were doing in the States before you came here."

The boys enjoyed their visit with her and thanked her for her gracious acceptance of the task.

September came and the American School, which Alcoa maintained in Via Bella, opened their school year—Bob, Cronan, Sean, Chris, Brigid and Hilary were enrolled there. Bob always left a little early to push Jack Nevins to school in his wheelchair—he had muscular dystrophy. The school day ended at noon; after lunch, when homework was completed, play began. Many days, a baseball game at the schoolyard, coached and refereed by Jack, was first on the agenda—he didn't tolerate any goofing off. Some days, if he thought the kids were taking too long doing their homework, he'd get someone to push him over to our house and get the kids working on it.

Camille was still too young for school—she became fast friends with the youngest girl, Babe, next door. She was the youngest of the Dutch family living there—her sisters also were in their school all morning.

The difference in language didn't deter them from becoming fast friends. After we moved to Paranam, their chauffeur would bring her there some mornings to play with Camille.

As the work of the courses progressed, Terry Jr. was having some trouble with his math course—that's how Michael Pulley (a girl: her mother had expected a boy) came into our life. She was spending some vacation time with her mother, an American living in Villa Bella. While she helped Terry, she occasionally stayed and had dinner with us. Michael had one sister and was totally amazed at the size of our family—she loved seeing everyone at the table.

She emitted a unique sound when startled or when emphasizing a point in her lively conversations at the dinner table—in our family affectionately known as a "Michael sound."

One day she announced:

"My mother and her husband will be gone this weekend; I want to make dinner for you at their house Saturday: dinner at six."

"Okay, we'll be there."

By early Saturday afternoon, she called and recruited Terry Jr. to come and help her; she was making Italian spaghetti and meatballs with salad and garlic bread—the amount of ingredients she was dealing with overwhelmed her. When we arrived at six, the water for the spaghetti had just been put on the stove.

"I'm so sorry I'm running a little late."

"That's okay, Michael, you're doing fine."

"I do have the garlic bread made—how about having that for appetizers?"

"That'll be fine."

At seven, everything was ready—we gathered around (not all fit at the table) ready to say prayers. At the same moment, a "Michael sound" was heard as her mother walked in the back door. It was quite evident by her mother's reaction that Michael had not told her of her plans.

"Michael, we decided to cut short our weekend. Go on with dinner; we've already eaten," she said as she picked her way through all the people in the room.

The look on Michael's face said it all. We went on with the dinner—it was delicious. She looked reassured as the plates came around for seconds. Yes, Terry Jr. stayed behind to help with the dishes.

One day I received a call from Steve Serdahely, who recently arrived in Suriname on an assignment for World Health.

"I was just talking with the consulate regarding the possibility of finding a high school for my children who are coming here. They told me that you have all the information I need."

I told him about the correspondence courses and what that entailed.

"Since I have you on the phone and you sound like a nice lady, I have another favor to ask: could you take care of our dog until the family arrives?"

He explained that they lived in Sri Lanka before accepting the assignment in Suriname. His family and their shipment went to their home in San Francisco; they planned to come to Suriname later—part of that shipment was a dog carrier with their dog, Leishe.

Steve came directly to Suriname; somehow the dog was put on the plane with him instead of going to San Francisco. Steve was staying in a hotel downtown—animals were not allowed: Leishe lived in the closet there at the present time.

"What kind of dog is it?"

"She's a Tibetan terrier."

Mmm, any dog from Tibet must be huge—what are we going to do with a huge dog at our house? But we can't leave her in a hotel closet.

"All right, we'll take care of her."

I gave Steve directions to our house—a little later, a car pulled into our driveway. I looked through the glass doors at the car and didn't see a dog peering out the window. Instead, Steve opened the back door, picked up a small carrier from the back seat and came to the door.

"Hello, Mrs. McCarthy, this is Leishe."

"But, she's so tiny—I thought she would be huge."

"In Tibet they have the large dog on guard below their house that's built on stilts—the terrier is in the house."

Steve explained that Leishe apparently was terrified of the noise of the jet engines on the plane—the trip was extremely long also. Now, as he opened the carrier, she streaked across the room to the underside of a cabinet in the dining room and ignored all urging to come out.

She stayed there several days; we placed food and water within her reach but she refused to come out while we were there. Then one day I saw her venture out—I was alone in the house and remained sitting in the chair in the living room, watching her. She slowly came to me, started sniffing my feet and finally looked up at me. She licked the hand I offered and that was it. She accepted the rest of the family in time—Jane became very attached to her.

Steve and his family later moved into a house a block from us—his wife, Laurel, came one day to take Leishe home. Leishe wasn't too happy to leave us. In fact, whenever I visited Laurel, Leishe got very excited, jumped into my lap and stayed there until I left.

With all the activity around our house, it was quite difficult for Terry Jr., Kevin and Rory to do their school work at their desks—there were so many interruptions.

Terry requested the use of one of the trailers located in the staff club area in Paranam for their schoolroom—Alcoa maintained these trailers for short-term American families; one was available at that time. His request was granted—this worked out well; the wife of one of the Americans living there was a teacher and qualified to give the tests to the boys. This was much more convenient than going to the consulate in Paramaribo to take the tests. The university agreed to the new arrangement so the transition was made.

The boys went to Paranam with Terry on Monday and returned with him Friday evening. During the week, they lived in the trailer and ate their meals at the staff club—the cooks there told us they never saw so much food disappear so fast in all their years there.

As I became more accustomed to driving in the city, I started taking note of the types of buildings there. The churches, government buildings and houses were modest in size and Dutch in character. Some really fine specimens of the architecture were the Government House, the Catholic cathedral, the mosque, the Court of Justice and the old Town Hall—the Cathedral is the largest wooden cathedral in the Western hemisphere. The cornerstone was laid January 30, 1883, and completed in July, 1885.

Suralco's managing director, Waldo Porter, lived in one of the old large wooden houses—the Corner House; it stood on the corner of Waterkant and Gravenstraat near the Government House.

Mr. Porter was a short wave radio enthusiast: when Thor Hyerdal ran into trouble with his first papyrus boat, Ra, in the Atlantic near the islands, Mr. Porter radioed Thor and told him he could send an Alcoa ship to help him. Thor thanked him but said he had help coming.

I liked learning the names of the streets, Brokapondalaan, Keizerstraat, Zwartenhovenbrugstraat, Steenbokkenijstraat, Heiligenweg, Saramaccastraat. There was a fairly large market place near the Suralco office where I usually shopped for produce. It was near the Pul-a-Pontse bridge. The bridge was so named because the Bush Negro had to pull pants over his loin cloth before entering town.

Periodically, I went to the huge market place downtown on the Suriname River. Among the fresh vegetables, my favorite was kouseband (meaning garter): a foot-long thin green bean. I liked buying the fresh-ground curry powder in the Hindustani section: the aroma permeated the area. Fresh fish from the Suriname River were also available—one, called koebie, had beautiful white solid stones behind the eyes which were used in making jewelry. I collected quite a few of them.

Meat was very expensive at the stores; we found a butcher shop near our home where we purchased a quarter of beef at a time: they cut and wrapped it for freezing. The cattle there were much smaller than those in the States: it was a reasonable amount for our small freezer.

Sundays were usually spent at the swimming pool in Paranam. After Mass and breakfast, we'd load into the van with swim suits, towels, etc., and take off. Sometimes we took the indirect roads: One was along the narrow and winding road some thirty miles south along the Suriname River. There we saw many Javanese homes with the little plots of rice and vegetables around the house. Another road, ten miles longer, was the Pad van Wanica and Meursweg roads. Many roadside stalls along this road featured Hindustani food like Roti met Kip: a Hindustani flat bread with chicken strips, cooked with hot, hot spices. Some of the vendors made special ones for those who couldn't tolerate that much spice.

The workers going to the Paranam Works had to travel these roads to the mine before Suralco built the new highway in 1969. The new highway followed a direct trail plotted to accommodate the high-voltage line carrying the Afobaka hydro-power from the Paranam substation to Paramaribo through mostly swampy land: this cut travel time in half for them.

The swimming pool at Paranam was always a welcome sight at the end of our trip. We usually ate dinner at the staff club and stayed for the movie shown there on Sunday nights.

Suriname was making plans to ordain its first Surinamer Roman Catholic bishop—they were very excited about it. We tried to get entrance cards for the ceremony to no avail. We resigned ourselves to watching it on TV.

The morning of the ceremony, as we left Mass, an usher followed our family from the church.

"I obtained an entrance card for the ceremony today but will be unable to go. Would one of you like to go?"

"Yes, of course; thank you so much."

I could hardly believe it. Our family decided I was the one to go. Many Surinamers, a people as culturally and racially varied as that found anywhere, attended the ceremony, many of whom were in native dress. An Indian lady wore a white chiffon sari embroidered with gold leaves, a lovely complement to her shining black hair and large dark eyes. Ahead of me was a Creole lady in her long starched cotton dress with matching anjisa, pleated and folded in her own fashion. Across the aisle was a Spanish lady, her black lace mantilla draped on her head, gracefully fanning herself with the matching lace fan. Over to the side, a Javanese lady was walking down the aisle in her ankle-length sarong with a tight lace bodice.

The decorations symbolized the bishop-to-be Aloysius Zichem's ancestry. A backdrop behind the altar of woven Javanese mats symbolized the native land of his mother. A decorative arrangement of anjissas, the starched bandanas worn by Creole women, were attached to the woven mats, representing his father's ancestry.

Thecla in market

Msgr. Zichem's father led the procession as the ceremony began—he walked alone because his wife did not live to see her son consecrated. He was followed by the Bishop of Paramaribo, the Cardinal and Archbishop of Utrecht, also the Nuncio and Apostolic Delegate for the Antilles, the Bishop of the Dominican Republic, the Bishop of British Guyana, the Bishop of Dutch Antilles, the Bishop of French Guyana, the Archbishop of Trinidad, the Bishop of Grenada and the Bishop-Elect Msgr. Aloysius Zichem. He looked so young and so small walking down the aisle and looked so alone as he prostrated himself on the floor in the middle of the sanctuary before the assembled bishops. Later, after he received his ring, his miter, and his staff, each of the bishops on the left side of the throne, moved one place to the left, vacating the chair next to the consecrating bishop—Bishop Zichem took his place in the center of his fellow Apostles.

Bishop Zichem with fellow bishops in the sanctuary of the cathedral

Then, visibly very deeply touched, Bishop Zichem came down by the altar and addressed the people. But his quick smile and splendid sense of humor soon came bubbling through—in a short time he had everyone smiling warmly.

The language was Dutch but I was able to follow the Mass and ceremony—a truly memorable day. Bishop Zichem ordained Waldie Wong Loi Sing, a Surinamer, to the priesthood a few months later on July 19, 1970.

The Alcoa News magazine from Pittsburgh carried my account of the ceremony in the September, 1970 issue. The cover of the magazine featured a picture of the World Trade Center under construction with this notation: "The color of the aluminum column covers that are the exterior of the World Trade Center has been described as a very light tan...Yamasaki beige...a warm silvery hue with just a touch of brown. While agreement in this area is elusive, most of the problems encountered in building the giant twin towers have been solved." When completed in 1973, the twin towers will soar 100 feet higher than the Empire State Building.

Although we usually attended Mass at the cathedral where the Mass was celebrated in the Dutch language, once a month, Father Donicie, a Dutch priest fluent in English, celebrated the Mass in English for the English-speaking Catholics. The Mass was held in the Catholic Missionary Headquarters in Paramaribo.

Brigid was old enough now to receive her First Holy Communion. Father Donicie made arrangements for her to receive instruction before receiving the sacrament.

I began looking for someone to sew a white dress for her—sewing was definitely not my forte. One of the American men, Mike Morris, had a local Javanese wife, Lou—she recommended her sister for the task. I brought some white linen material to her shop: the result was an exquisitely simple dress. A short length of lace served as her veil. She received Our Lord for the first time at the English Mass celebrated by Father Donicie.

The following year, the same arrangements were made for Hilary for his First Holy Communion—another American, Bruce Deci, celebrated with him.

When Camille was ready to receive Holy Communion for the first time, she also received her instructions at the Catholic Missionary Headquarters. Lou's sister was no longer around to make her dress—Mrs. Nevins, an American, came to the rescue and made the dress for her: a beautiful simple white silk dress. She also wore a short lace veil.

Jane usually rode the bus to and from our house every day; she was running late finishing up one day so I decided to take her home. Brigid, Hilary and Camille were with me. The streets were very crowded at that time of day— on the return trip, a short distance from our turnoff into Villa Bella, a city bus stopped suddenly in front of me. I slammed on the brakes and stopped with my bumper just rubbing the bumper of the bus—a truck behind me hit my back bumper enough to bend it a little.

The company told us, when we first arrived, if an American was involved in an accident, the local people really go after them. We were told to just remain quiet and respectful, which I did.

The bus driver and the driver behind me were yelling at me in Dutch and Taki-Taki—I gathered they were telling me I had to stay right there while they called the police. They went across the street to the bakery to use the phone— traffic was really snarled. A police car with two officers arrived; one officer, who spoke some English, came into our van and said he would accompany me in the van to the police station.

"We live a block from here; may I take the children home first?"

"Yes, I'll go with you," he said as he got into the van.

The children were very upset seeing me go off with the officer; I knew they'd be all right at home with the older boys.

When we arrived at the police station, I tried to show them that there was no damage to the front bumper but the back one was damaged by the truck hitting me. I was taken inside the station and an officer started filling out a report.

"May I call the Suralco office?"

I was given permission—a gentleman at the office, who dealt with this type of thing, said he'd be right over. When he arrived and spoke with the officers, he approached me.

"Let's go out to your van."

"Okay, you'll see there's only damage to the back bumper."

"I know, however, they say that is old damage and not caused today. I just want to let you know what's going on and why they are making out a report. Just go and sign it and we will take care of it."

"I guess I'll have to do as you say."

I signed it and was on my way home.

Terry decided to start taking flying lessons—hopefully, that would help take his mind off his work. He was in charge of mine production: the work was quite intense. Short days were twelve hours long, fourteen to sixteen were standard. The mine was in very bad shape mostly because of drainage—it was below sea level.

When an airplane and instructor became available at the Aero Club in November, he took advantage of it. The first lesson lasted a half hour—it was so demanding he thought of nothing else for almost a full day: it was worth the effort. His instructor was a mechanic/instructor, Bob Smith, who had flown in the Marine Corps during WWII—he was his ground school instructor too.

Getting flying instructions was essentially a matter of having the instructor, the plane, the weather, the student and the spirit to do it, all come together in the same place. Terry's log book showed that in a four-month period, he had accumulated 16.25 hours. When he was ready to solo, each time he tried, something would happen causing a two- to three-week gap in flying time—the only reasonable solution—buy an airplane. So the search was on.

With a subscription to *Trade-A-Plane*, Terry started looking for planes to buy. Suralco scheduled him to do some training development work at Alcoa's mining operations in Jamaica so he flew to Miami and Ft. Lauderdale to check out some ads he had seen in the publication before going to Jamaica. Now he had a list of planes to look at when we returned to the States for the McCarthy family reunion in 1971.

The Aero Club had a Piper PA 18 Super Cub in their hangar—it was disassembled for the installation of new fabric. The members of the club decided instead to put it up for sale. The plane served in the Dutch air force during World War II—a military version with a "greenhouse canopy"; it still had camouflage paint on the fabric fuselage. We decided to purchase it—no, not a plane for flying, just to work on. There was the understanding the plane stayed in the hangar until we found a place for it.

When we later moved to a house on stilts in Paranam, it was parked under our house, the wings hanging from the rafters. Here it was lovingly stripped of the fabric and reduced to just the frame. I frequently climbed into it—I liked the feel of the joy stick—I think I could've flown that plane. Terry told me to choose the colors for the interior—aqua blue and white was my choice.

When I took the receipt for the purchase of the plane to the government office that dealt with that sort of thing to register it, I remembered the long wait at the post office to pick up the correspondence courses. I brought reading material along to fill in the time. I walked into the office, showed the gentleman what I had and what I requested, and within a few minutes, I left the office with all the documentation in my hand—airplanes were easy to buy down there.

When we left Suriname in 1973, the plane was taken apart, boxed and shipped back to the States. Terry went to New York, rented a truck and picked up the shipment—in winter conditions, he brought it to Elmwood, Illinois, where we lived at that time. From there it traveled to Tucson, Arizona—the wings and fuselage were stored in a shed in the backyard, the struts decorated our bedroom wall for a time. Later, our son, Chris, bought it and attempted to restore it—ultimately, he sold it when he moved to another state. Hopefully, some day we'll track it down to see how it's doing.

I sat in on some of the ground school lessons Terry took and took a short flight with Bob after one of the sessions: flying was second nature to him. That prompted the poem below.

That flight brought back my desire to fly in an open cockpit all the more. I hadn't completely forgotten about that—just sidetracked for a while. I'll get back to that.

Why Fly?

I asked you: "Was it fun to fly?"
"Was it fun to drive?" you asked in reply
As if there's no difference between earth and sky.

Then on the last run, my chance came
And as we flew, it was not a pilot and plane
For they moved together—they were the same.

So you can tell me again—"so what if I fly"
But I won't believe you and you'll know why
'Cause I've been with you up there in the sky.

Each year, Queen Juliana's birthday was celebrated with a formal dance at the staff club. This first year, as Terry and I came down the receiving line at the dance, several people looked at Terry and then asked me: "Who did you bring to the dance?" "I found him and thought he was quite handsome so I brought him along." (They only saw him in work clothes and hard hat a good part of that first year.)

A while later he motioned to me.

"I want to be at the mine at 10:00 when the shift changes—you want to come along?"

"Sure, that sounds interesting."

Off we went down the mine road in our VW bug to the open pit where the shift was changing—quite a strange sight seeing Terry walking down into the pit in his tux and a hard hat along with all the men starting their shift.

He returned to the car looking none the worse for wear, threw the hard hat into the back seat, and we returned to the dance.

Now, we would soon be celebrating our first Christmas here. It was celebrated quite differently—St. Nicholas brings all the gifts on his feast, the sixth of December: he arrives, dressed like a bishop, on a boat in the Suriname River.

As we started our Christmas shopping, we found that most of the toys in the stores are the small battery-driven cars and trucks; our boys liked the big metal tanks, dozers, scrapers, etc. For the girls, there were little cases available for Barbie dolls and their clothes but no dolls in them—I filled the cases with material and trimmings so we could make clothes for the girls' old dolls.

I liked going into the gold and silver jewelry shops to watch the men making the beautiful pieces of jewelry—some of it so intricate and thread thin; other necklaces held nuggets of gold, coarse and unfinished.

Each year, a Christmas sale was held at the rehabilitation center where hand-designed Christmas cards besides the regular articles were sold—they depended a lot on Christmas sales. I solicited the help of the American ladies—we brought and sold cakes and coffee at the sale to help in their profits.

Christmas Eve, Santa Claus in the person of Pete Grayler, came "ho-ho-ing" into the house. He had no need of padding for his suit or a change of personality—his laugh was infectious: a perfect Santa Claus.

However, our Christmas tree left a little to be desired: a large branch of a tropical pine tree, held up by rope tied to the decorative divider between the living and dining rooms. The crib was in place in the living room with Mary, Joseph, the cow and donkey inside; the shepherds with their sheep outside, all awaiting the arrival of Baby Jesus. This part of Christmas never changed.

Paramaribo really celebrated on New Year's Eve. One of the local families across the street from us started the fireworks at midnight—they weren't little pop-ups and sparklers—they were the real thing. When they finished, we could hardly see the houses around us—the smoke was stifling. Going to Mass the next morning, we saw the cloud of smoke hanging over the whole city.

Wonder what the New Year will bring us in this new land.

MAP OF SURINAME

By Terry McCarthy, Sr.

Note! Black dots denote locations

Chapter V

Samara Revisited

Our New Year began with a new addition to the family—Flint, a multi-colored macaw. One of the men Terry was training, Larry MacArthur, brought Flint to Terry. He found the parrot at a Bush Negro village. Flint's wing was injured permanently, which made flight impossible. He ruled from the perch on the back patio. Only a large lizard who roamed the yards frightened Flint: his raucous calling of danger could wake the dead. He loved the rain; when put on a branch of the tree during a rain storm, his screeching and flapping made everyone laugh.

Family photo, Sean holding Flint

Sean was Flint's favorite—when he saw Sean, he'd start his little dance waiting for him to come and hold out his hand so he could perch on it. "Da," the Dutch word for hello, was the only word he spoke. He slept under Sean's bed at night.

As time passed, Flint forgot more and more that he was supposed to be a bird—he made himself a part of the family. Sean brought him into the house when we were getting ready to celebrate Kevin's birthday; as Kevin was lighting the candles on the cake, Flint walked to his chair, looked up at him, saying over and over "Da, da." As we started singing "Happy Birthday," he yelled at the top of his lungs, pupils dilating the whole time—of course, he ate a piece of the cake.

Jane was afraid of him—if he just heard her voice he started his muttering; if he was on the floor at the time, he'd march up to her and try to bite her ankles. I always made sure he was on his perch on the back patio when Jane was around.

M. Rambharos, another of the men Terry trained, gave us the opportunity to experience something entirely new. He invited us to his son's wedding—the Hindustani wedding was celebrated for five nights. In preparation, the first evening we went with Rambharos to the home of the bride-to-be, B. Ramesar—her family lived in an area surrounded by rice paddies where there was no electricity. Flaming torches lighted the way along the path to the house. We gathered in the lamplight of the home: the girl's father gave permission to T.L.S. Rambharos for his daughter's hand in marriage.

The next night everyone went to bless the house where the couple would live. The celebrants danced and chanted as roasted rice was strewn about blessing the house;

The third night everyone gathered at the groom's house—the men stayed below (the house was on stilts) and the women gathered above in the house. There, one woman played a two-stringed sitar and chanted a song while the rest of us took turns doing a dance—yes, I did too, which brought on much laughter as I tried to imitate what they had done. I don't know what the men did below during that time.

The fourth night everyone shared a meal at the home of the groom—Terry Jr., Kevin, Rory and Bob helped serve. The food was served with roti (very similar to the tortilla) and eaten with the hands—our family was served food with much less spice than theirs; they also provided spoons for us.

70

The fifth afternoon, an elaborate ceremony took place at the groom's home. He was seated on a small throne as his mother, dressed in her sari, wound a long strip of material and formed the turban on her son's head which matched the robe he was wearing. It was sad, though, because the mother may not attend the actual wedding ceremony.

The ceremony took place in a large tent near the bride's home. It began when the father of the bride and father of the groom, seated outside a smaller tent inside the larger one, bartered gifts back and forth. Then the bride came out of the small tent, dressed in a beautiful pink sari and the wedding ceremony took place.

A meal followed—the members of the wedding party had different plates and cups. The plates as well as the cups were metal (bronze-looking), the plate was shaped like a shallow bowl; the cup had a round bottom and a thin neck which flared out on the top. *Rambharos gave Terry one of the sets used that night—he still uses the plate every day; the cup, however, never lost the metallic taste to its contents when used. No manner of soaking removed that taste.*

The guests were then treated to a very long play—the ornate costumes of the participants helped depict the story of the origins of their culture (all the roles were played by men). The play went on until daylight. Our young ones napped at times in our van during that time. It always amazed me how the men drank scotch from regular water glasses and didn't show signs of intoxication as the evening progressed.

The first few months of the year passed rather swiftly and as the school year was winding down, we began making vacation plans—Alcoa had a policy that expatriates vacation somewhere outside the country once a year. Terry planned to take a jungle trip in August to the interior of Suriname at the Brazilian border. Some of the children and I planned to go to Costa Rica to visit friends. We wanted to arrive there early in May before the rainy season started.

I contacted the Alcoa Steamship office for tickets regarding the intended trip—Bob, Cronan, Sean, Christopher, Brigid, Hilary, Camille and I were on the list. We received the tickets to fly BIWI (British West Indies). According to the itinerary, we'd overnight in Bridgetown, Barbados, continuing west from there to San Jose, Costa Rica.

At Zanderij airport, we kissed Dad and the three older boys good-bye and boarded the plane. It was nice to settle down and relax after the rather hectic two weeks of finishing up school here in Paramaribo and packing for our three-week trip, most of it on the Nicoyan Peninsula of Costa Rica.

We were soon on our way and after a short stop in Georgetown, Guyana, we were heading for Trinidad. We couldn't resist getting off the plane there and checking everything out. I was counting noses as we gathered to board the plane again—a gentleman approached me and said: "I don't suppose you know me but I know quite a lot about you. I had the pleasure of being seated alongside one of your children on the plane."

What he heard must not have been too bad for he didn't seem afraid to talk to me. Our little visit with him was interrupted by the announcement of our departing flight. We started out while the three islanders wearing BIWI hats and jackets stamped with their insignia strummed guitars and sang farewell. All was not ready aboard, however, and we were sent back into the building—the islanders stopped playing and singing. I continued my chat with the gentleman.

He was Brian Jones from London—his company, Jones Ross & Co. Ltd., dealt with silk and cotton hand-loomed and printed fabrics. He came to Suriname to check out the Indonesian batik.

Printing the fabric involved quite a process. Each particular design in the fabric that was not to be dyed was coated with wax during the dyeing process. The finished fabric was beautiful and was sold in sarong lengths: the distinct smell of the wax remained even after all the washings. Brian was very impressed with the quality of the fabric.

"Mr. Jones, maybe you can help us with something. We have a Garrard turntable that is not working—it is impossible to replace that part for it in Suriname."

"I know the manufacturer in London; I'm familiar with the part you need. I'll be glad to get it and send it to you."

We exchanged addresses—one never knows what business transactions can occur because your son likes to talk with people. The flight departure was again announced, the islanders once more bade us farewell in song and we boarded the plane, bound for Barbados. Once aloft, the stewardess gave me eight cards to fill out for immigration at our destination. If there is any one deterring factor in traveling with that many, that might be it. Names, dates of birth, etc., and this occurs in every country you visit overnight.

When we arrived home later that month the part for our turntable was there. I sent a check to Mr. Jones; he sent it back with a letter stating it was "too difficult to discount this here, and suggest that I contact you when I am in Suriname which I hope will be in January." Regretfully, we never met him again.

"Boy, Mom, we'll have the rest of the afternoon to swim in the ocean," one of the boys exclaimed as we sailed on through customs and immigration in the terminal.

"I'm going to reconfirm our reservations for our continuing flight to San Jose tomorrow and then we'll be off to the hotel."

I went to the ticket counter and gave my tickets to the agent. She looked at the tickets, looked at me with a strange look, excused herself and went into the back room. She came back still looking perplexed.

"Mrs. McCarthy, the ticket reads San Jose, but the flight number listed goes east to Amsterdam, Holland. Barbados is the easternmost island in the Caribbean and there never has been any flight west from here to Costa Rica. If you like to go to Holland, we will honor the ticket because that flight number is listed."

I was stunned, to say the least. *I learned later that this type of thing was not unusual for the Alcoa Steamship Company in Paramaribo.*

"There's no way I want to go to Amsterdam with seven children and no hotel reservations. What is the alternative?"

"You can either go through Venezuela in South America to San Jose or go through Miami. Either way will require an extra night here at the hotel to book you on another flight."

Staying another night here would necessitate more cash. Hopefully, I could get into a bank in Miami that would give me the cash I needed from our checking account in Texas.

"I'll take the flight through Miami."

"We'll call your hotel and book you an extra day."

"Thank you."

The Crane Hotel at St. Philip, Barbados, was beautiful and very old—it had the look of a castle with thick walls and wooden floors. It stood on a rock prominence about fifty feet above the Atlantic with an absolutely gorgeous view of the ocean.

In the afternoon, we walked down the path and long staircase to the beach. We didn't swim there though because the waves near the rock prominence were too wild. (The beach farther down was filled with patrons of the hotels right on the beach.) Instead, we sat in the sand watching a young man diving into the ocean from a ledge partway up the rock prominence—apparently, some of the tourists paid him to do it. I don't know how he was always able to dive into the deep pool of water among all the rocks.

The Black Panthers were holding a conference at one of the hotels right on the beach. One of the members came and sat by us and started asking all sorts of questions about us and where we were staying. I did not feel comfortable with that conversation so we excused ourselves and started the long trek back up the steps to our hotel.

After dinner that evening, Brigid, Hilary, Camille and I were sitting in our room enjoying the beauty of it: the old wooden floor and walls and the intricately carved wooden headboards on the beds. Cronan knocked and came into the room.

"Mom, Bob is sitting on the other side of the fence on the rock ledge—it looks pretty scary."

My heart skipped a beat as I visualized the scene.

"Cronan, make sure the other boys stay in their room—I don't think I'll accomplish anything by going there; he knows beforehand what I think about it."

Bob came to the room later and apologized; I let it be known I would tolerate no more of that.

Our stay at the hotel was very pleasant. The second day was Sunday, Mothers' Day. The front desk arranged for a van to come by and take us to Mass. There was, however, a misunderstanding in directions: we attended an Anglican Mass instead of a Catholic Mass that day. The Liturgy was similar but it was quite evident that is was not the same. The church was very old and beautiful; grave markers on the floor indicated graves of very early residents, many of them seamen.

The van was waiting for us as we came out—I told the driver it was not a Catholic church.

"I'm sorry—I thought I followed the directions given me."

"That's okay, I'm sure you did."

The lady at the desk explained later that the names of the churches were very similar and a short distance apart: that was the reason for the mistake.

A wonderful special Mothers' Day dinner was served that evening. The dining room looked out over the ocean: it was necessary to have a glass windbreak on the balcony wall—the breeze was a bit too much. All in all, it was a lovely day.

Monday morning, we headed for the airport—we had breakfast at the restaurant there. As I approached the register to pay the bill, a gentleman came alongside me.

"May I please pay the bill for you and your children—it was a pleasure to see such well-behaved and polite children,"

"Indeed you may—thank you."

As we approached Puerto Rico, an announcement was made that everyone and their luggage would be going through customs there. I pressed the call button and the stewardess approached.

"We're on a continuing flight to San Jose through Miami."

"That makes no difference—you go through customs in Puerto Rico."

As we deplaned in San Juan, we heard another announcement.

"Will the mother traveling with seven children come and see me, please."

We saw the gentleman making the announcement and walked up to him.

"Please stay here with me and as your luggage comes out, identify it and we will transfer it to your flight going to Costa Rica."

"Thank you, sir, you have made my day. I need to get to a bank in Miami before they close."

We continued on to Miami. I made it to a bank inside just in time—the man there heard my story.

"What is the name of a director at your bank in Texas—I'll call him; you can speak to him; if he okays it, we'll give you the money."

Luckily, I remembered one who knew Terry very well: the call was made to Texas. The gentleman there was so glad to hear from us and wanted to know all about Terry and his work in Suriname—I finally reminded him what I needed; he graciously okayed my request—the check was cashed.

As our flight to San Jose was ready to board, an announcement came over the intercom that a child was missing from a family scheduled for the flight: the flight would be delayed until the child was found. There was a scramble everywhere around the boarding area.

"Let's get on board, kids, so we're out of the way of all this."

We settled in and waited. Finally, a mother, father and a little girl came on board looking a bit disheveled. A gentleman from the airline followed them to their seats and then he approached me.

"My apologies to you—when I first heard there was a child missing, I thought it had to be the mother traveling with seven children that was missing one of the children. Instead, it was a family with one child."

"Your apologies are accepted."

"I'm going on this flight also—I have arranged for your children to be fed; then the stewardess will bed them down in the empty seats so they can sleep the rest of the way. Then, with your permission, we will have dinner."

"Thank you very much. I accept your invitation."

What a dinner—wine, steaks and the works.

At the stops along the way, I heard the soft lyrical tones of the Spanish language spoken as passengers and baggage were exchanged: so different from the harsh, guttural tones of the Dutch language spoken in Suriname.

In San Jose, the long ride in the taxi to the hotel proved as hair-raising as we remembered it—the driver spent most of the time looking at us instead of the road: he thought Camille's red hair and freckles were beautiful and didn't stop talking about it.

Morning found us back at the airport for the Lacsa flight to the little town of Nicoya, where we lived several years before: Then the small single-engine plane at the Nicoya airport took us to the grass runway of our final destination: Playa Samara. It looked just as beautiful as it always had. Arriving by plane gave us a more breathtaking view of the whole area—we could see the extent of the coral reef and the beautiful curve of the white sand beach.

This was very different from the journey by bus we experienced when we lived in Nicoya: the two-hour ride in the bus with the windows open. Dust coated us and everyone and everything on board: we looked as though we had make-up on. After that long dusty ride, what a glorious sight it was to see the blue, blue water stretching out to the horizon. Then, within seconds after our arrival at Pension de Carmen, we'd down a cold bottle of soda, put on our swimsuits and let the waves wash off the dust.

Now, we stayed at Pension de Carmen as before—she and Nicolas were so happy to see us again. They remembered Camille as a baby and were delighted to see the change in her: her red hair enchanted everyone. The rooms were the same as we remembered them: plain wooden floors, cots, poles to hang up clothes, only wooden shutters on the windows. The children went off in all directions to check out everything.

"Mom, look—the monkeys are taking their siestas in the mango tree in the backyard just like they always did; they look so funny lying on their tummies with arms and legs draping down."

"I'm sure their tummies are full with all those mangos to feast on."

"The tide's out now—we'll go see all the pools with the pretty fish."

"Don't stay out too long; Carmen will have dinner ready soon."

Carmen laughed as she kept refilling the bowls of black beans and rice along with the chicken and tortillas—what appetites the sea air gave us. After dinner, she told the children they could help her get the ladder to place against the trunk of the mango tree. When it was in place, the chickens started climbing up to the lowest branch to perch in safety for the night. Cronan said: "I remember doing this when we were living here in Costa Rica."

We took a walk along the beach as the sun was setting—soon the sound of the surf would lull us to sleep: what beauty God lavishes on us. As we returned to the *pension*, we heard the generator start up to provide the power for the single bulb in our rooms—the cots looked very inviting after a long day.

We woke to the smell of tortillas frying. They were still made very early in the morning when the crude corn was ground in a hand grinder—the corn had soaked all night in water mixed in wood ashes (lye): the lye mixture loosens the hull of the corn so it rinses away; it is rinsed many, many times before it is ground three times, mixed with a little water and fried: the best tortillas we've ever tasted. They served them warm with a wonderful combination of scrambled eggs, black beans and rice.

After breakfast, we decided to explore along the beach and go swimming later.

"Mom, let's go see our favorite tree near the stream flowing into the ocean."

"Okay, that's a nice walk."

It was a real Swiss Family Robinson tree with many trunks that covered a huge area—It always provided entertainment any time of the day. We could hear the occupants long before we got there. Cronan and Sean were up ahead of us.

"Boy, it's really lively this morning—monkeys are everywhere."

"Look at the lizards racing around looking for food in the maze of roots."

Camille didn't remember seeing the tree before: she was so excited at the number of different animals living together in one tree.

"Mom, look at the parrots up in the branches—they get along with all the other animals."

"I guess that's because there's all types of food available for them."

"It's really fun watching all of them."

"They're probably having as much fun talking to each other about the funny two-legged creatures staring at them from all angles."

"Let's get back to the *pension* now and head for the water."

Carmen still had her magic touch in the sauce she served with the lobster some fishermen brought in just in time for lunch. After a little *siesta*, we were ready for a swim again. Nicolas served the cold Fanta Uva and Fanta Naranja, the local grape and orange soda, to us when we came in and found our favorite chairs to watch the activities around the *pension*.

"The pigs are sloshing around in the ditch where the wash-water is draining."

"They won't be there long—here comes Carmen to chase them out."

"Look, some chickens are dusting themselves in that pile of ashes from the wood fire: Carmen said that helps them get rid of lice."

"Mom, remember when Rory got Kevin, Terry and Bob to throw clods of dirt up in the mango tree so the monkeys would throw mangoes down for them?"

"I do—it worked like a charm."

The backyard was always full of surprises.

One afternoon, the small plane landed on the beach when the tide was out. A tall gentleman emerged—from the sound of his voice I deducted he was an American: his Spanish had that ring to it. After the plane left, he stood looking at the exposed reef for a while and then approached me.

"Are those your children out on the reef?"

"Yes, they are, they spend a lot of time out there."

"I'm a marine biologist from Cornell University studying sea anemones along the Central American coast—I'll have fun with the children for a few days."

"I'm sure they'll enjoy every bit of it."

And that they did—they anxiously waited each day for the tide to expose the reef and they slowly returned with the incoming tide. There were always tales to tell.

"Mom, he shows us so many interesting things—today, we saw something that grows in the water that's used in some types of toothpaste."

"He taught us the names of those bright-colored fish we like to watch."

"We took him to that spot where we found the octopus—he liked to watch it squirt ink if our hand came too close."

"He liked the part that looks like a castle with a moat around it."

It was a sad bunch that stood on the beach a few days later waving as the plane took their friend away to another beach.

On a bright sunny afternoon, after eating lunch, I sat on the verandah in my favorite chair—through half-closed eyes, I saw three horsemen emerging from a grove of trees at the furthest curve of the beach to the left of the *pension*. I watched as they slowly grew larger and then finally rode by to the outside bar at the *pension* next door.

One rider was a young Hispanic—the other two, older men. The young man looked delighted when he saw the children swimming and riding the waves into shore. He spoke to the other men and then went to talk to the children. Soon he came back, got his horse, and let the older children take rides on it. I noticed that the older men never took their eyes off the young man—they watched him constantly. The young man approached me.

"Excuse me, may the younger children ride on my horse while I lead it? I'll be very careful with them."

"You have my permission."

"Thank you."

He seemed very well educated and spoke English with hardly any accent. He was thoroughly enjoying his visit with the children.

Carmen came out and joined me.

"Carmen, who is that young man out there talking with the children?"

"I don't know—I've never seen him before."
"How about those two men next door—they watch him constantly."
"I don't know them either."

The men next door soon called out to the young man—he immediately shook hands with the children, came and said good-bye to Carmen and me and rode off with the men.

Carmen watched them leave.

"I have heard there is a large beautiful house farther down the coast that is well-guarded; no one here knows who lives there."

"Well, I'm glad we had this brief encounter with the young man—he looked happy being with the children."

Later, the children said he didn't talk about himself. They knew he was well-educated and aware of things happening in the rest of the world. They thoroughly enjoyed their visit with him.

Then it was time to take the plane back to Nicoya and from there to San Jose—I like taking off from San Jose: the plane circles to gain altitude to cross the mountains and affords us a nice last look at the city. We took the Panama–Caracas–Trinidad route back to Suriname.

May of 1972, Cronan, Sean, Chris, Brigid, Hilary, Camille and I went back to Samara for our vacation. This time, we requested the flight to San Jose by way of Venezuela and Panama on Pan Am. We stopped at Trinidad, then Caracas—from Caracas, as we neared Panama, the captain spoke on the intercom.

"I noticed that we have some young children on board; I asked for permission to descend to a lower altitude so they can get a good look at the Panama Canal."

That was so thoughtful of him—we were surprised to see how narrow the passages for the ships were. We asked the stewardess to thank the captain for us.

We stayed overnight in Panama and went by a smaller plane to San Jose—what a gorgeous view we had of the countryside: large waterfalls looked static from the air but beautiful: we could imagine the roar of the water and feel the mist from them.

In the smaller plane, the children and I were not grouped together—Hilary was sitting with a gentleman toward the front of the plane. When we landed, I remained seated until Hilary came down the aisle. The gentleman he'd been sitting with stopped by my seat as he deplaned.

"I enjoyed my visit with your son. I know a lot more about you than you can ever imagine—it was a delightful trip."

Children and mirrors tell the truth.

There was a lot of excitement and activity at Samara when we arrived—a cement runway was in the process of replacing the grass runway. A man with a dozer, from the Ministerio de Transporte in San Jose, was dozing down trees and brush to widen the runway.

As soon as we were settled into our rooms, the older boys were off to watch the work at the airport. They were familiar with that type of work—they saw their dad doing it many times: they enjoyed every bit of it.

Some palm trees were being removed almost every day—we had heart of palm with Carmen's special sauce served with it at most of our meals: that wasn't hard to take.

I tried riding a horse again this time—when we lived in Nicoya a few years before I had a wild ride on a horse up a mountain and didn't think I'd ever try it again. This time I rode to the next beach a few miles away. The tide was in so we had to stick to the shoreline, which made it quite a bit longer—I didn't sit much the next couple of days after that trip.

Then the rains came—early this year. The bus stopped coming because the road washed out; the small plane wasn't available; Sunday, there was no way to get to Mass. A small ship came into the bay delivering provisions for the people living here.

"Carmen, do they take passengers on that ship?"

"Yes, they do."

"If we go with them we could get to Mass in Puntarenas—I remember where the cathedral is there."

"No, no, please don't do that; it's too dangerous with all the children."

I took her advice.

We experienced something new here at Samara this time. They called it *Mala Noche*—as the tide came in, the waves came all the way up to the *pension* leaving pools of water in the yard. It was a little scary. The water in the shower was salty so showers didn't do any good. It was time to leave.

Sean, Chris, and Hilary went out on the reef for one last time. A high sheer cliff protruded into the reef near Samara, dividing the reef in front of the *pension* from the part lining the more rugged coast. Most of the larger pools of water were on the other side of the cliff from the *pension*: that's where the boys went. I watched the tide returning; there was no sign of the boys coming around the cliff. I started running toward the reef calling as I ran.

"Dona Thecla, please slow down—you'll get sick running like that."

"Carmen, I've got to get to the kids." She was running beside me now. Soon the rocks of the reef made it impossible to run anymore. Then we saw them coming around the corner, the small waves splashing at their feet. Sean was limping badly but we knew they were safe now.

"I slipped on a rock and got a bad cut on the heel of my foot: that slowed us down."

"Oh, it's so good to see all of you."

We helped Sean hobble the rest of the way back: the waves were splashing on our thighs as we reached the sand. Carmen had everything we needed to bandage his wound.

Nicolas had radioed for the small plane to come to pick us up the next day—they said they would come. It rained during the night; the little stream between the beach and the runway was flowing. As the plane approached, Nicolas put Sean on his back; he and the rest of us waded across the stream and were ready to board when the plane taxied up to us.

We spent the next few days in Nicoya at Hotel Ali—the shower felt good. We walked up the hill from the town to INVU, to see the house where we had lived. The neighbors came out to meet us and introduce us to additions to their families. They told us that our dear friend, Maria, moved downtown in Nicoya—they gave us directions to her house there.

"Hola, Maria."

"Hola, dona Thecla."

It was just like the old days when I passed her house and greeted her—we had quite a reunion. We met some of her children and their husbands and her grandchildren. She still made tortillas every day and soon served them with avocados: she knew how we loved them.

Later at the hotel, Jose came to visit us on his way home from school—his mother, Avelina, gave birth to him while she was working for us when we lived here: he spent a lot of time with us then. He still had those large dark eyes that melt your heart. He showed us his schoolwork: it gave evidence that he was a bright little boy. He sat beside me explaining his work; once he gave me a long thoughtful look as though he remembered me: he was about two years old when we left.

Even though my Spanish was not too good and his English about the same, we managed to communicate.

"My mother moved to San Jose with the rest of the children but I wanted to stay here in Nicoya with my grandmother."

"Does your aunt, Maestra Nydia, still live here too?"

"Yes, she does—she still teaches in high school. She has a car now and also owns a small farm outside of town."

"Give them my regards when you go home."

A little later, Jose returned with an invitation to have dinner with them. We accepted and enjoyed a delicious black bean, rice and chicken meal. After dinner, Nydia motioned me aside.

"Would you consider adopting Jose and taking him with you now? I think it would be good for him to be with your family. I talked to Avelina about it and she is in agreement."

I was a little stunned.

"Nydia, I can't make that decision without talking to my husband; I don't know if the U.S. Embassy would permit it either."

"Would you please try to find out if it's possible?—I think it would be best for Jose."

"Yes, I will try."

The next day I placed a call to Terry from a phone in the telephone office in town. He also was a little stunned at first but said he thought we could handle it. I placed a call to the U.S. Embassy in San Jose and reached the person who could help me. She took down all the information.

"Please call back tomorrow—I'll see what I can do for you."

"Thank you."

When I returned the call the next day, she said it was possible to get the necessary papers processed—Avelina lived in San Jose and could come with me to the consulate to sign the papers.

When I went to see Nydia at their home later that day to give her the information, her mother was very upset. It was quite evident they were not in agreement regarding Jose. The grandmother gave me a pleading look.

"I cannot let you take Jose away—I'd be guilty of sin; he'd be in a different country; he's not old enough to make that decision."

Nydia was furious and told her mother she was foolish not giving Jose the chance to go with us. Ultimately, I knew I couldn't do that to his grandmother—she took care of him as a baby when Avelina lived with her; Jose chose not to go with his mother when she moved to San Jose. She cried in my arms when I told her of my decision.

We left Nicoya and spent the night in San Jose. At the airport the next day, customs said they wanted to open and check all the little Pan Am bags the children were carrying. When they opened the first bag, which still had a damp swimsuit in it (we couldn't wash them anywhere or dry them since we'd been at Samara). When they got a whiff of that bag they decided to forego opening the rest of the bags.

We looked back at San Jose sparkling in the sunlight as we circled inside the mountains to gain altitude and were on our way back to Paramaribo via Venezuela: We spent a night at the Pan Am House in Trinidad—another completely different culture, home to the steel band: a new rhythm in the music and a new sound in the English spoken there.

We always liked Pan Am Airline—they were so courteous and did extra things for the children.

After our return to the States from Suriname, while living in Illinois, I returned to Samara to purchase a small plot of land from Carmen. We rode the bus to Nicoya to make out the purchase papers at her lawyer there. The bank in Nicoya didn't want to make the financial transaction right then so we took the bus to San Jose (she didn't like to fly).

I loved the bus ride—it brought back so many memories of our first trip to Nicoya in the '60s. The bus driver had the radio on—Carmen and I knew most of the songs: she sang the songs in Spanish and I sang them in English at the same time. Everyone on the bus joined in—a real holiday affair. She enjoyed her stay at the hotel in San Jose—I woke to her singing in the shower. I could hear her turn off the water different times while in the shower—they are so concerned about conserving water on the peninsula where she lived. After our transaction at the bank, she left on the bus and I on the plane.

On my return trip to Illinois, Lacsa stopped at Cayman Island. As we prepared to leave, a police car drove up to the steps of the plane—a man in handcuffs surrounded by plainclothes men came on board and occupied the front seats of the cabin. The stewardess told me the man in handcuffs traveling with them was involved in the big Brinks robbery in the States recently—he was apprehended on the island with his part of the money.

When we arrived in Miami, they departed the plane first. News people were everywhere with cameras flashing. I waited until last to deplane—the terminal area was a zoo.

Carmen had given me a bag of mangos for the children—the man at customs said that was a "no-no."

"I didn't think I could bring them in and told Carmen that but she said she remembered how the kids loved them and insisted that I take them."

"I'm sorry—but I will take them home and give them to my children."

"Thank you so much."

After our return home to Paranam, we all went to the local clinic for our yearly physical. Alcoa had a company policy of requiring a complete physical each year for every member of the families living overseas. Most of the families returned to the States on the one-month home leave—we didn't do that this year; consequently, the physical was done at the local clinic.

The doctor at the clinic called a few days later—the x-ray of my kidneys showed a dark spot on the right kidney. He wanted to use a scope to check it out.

I was scheduled into the hospital on Friday for the procedure to be done the following Monday.

"Why do I need to go there that far in advance when you said it is a simple procedure?"

"I want to make sure there is a room available for you."

I was quite apprehensive about the whole thing to begin with—this long stay didn't help. I wandered around the hospital those three days trying to keep my mind off what was in store. Luckily, I found a Dutch gentleman, who worked for Suralco and spoke English, who was in the same situation—we sat out on the veranda at times to pass away the time.

Monday morning, I was given a shot to make me drowsy. Then I was told to walk with the nurse down to the OR—that was quite an accomplishment. There, I sat in a chair outside the OR to await my turn. Finally, they gave me another shot, put me on a gurney and rolled me into the OR.

I could hear what everyone was saying but did not have the ability to speak because of the effects of the shot. My five-foot-nine-inch frame was a little more than the nurses wanted to lift onto the table. I heard them discussing this. The doctor told them: "Tell her to get on by herself—these Americans do anything once."

I tried to tell them what I thought of them but no sound came out. Surprisingly, after the procedure, they did take me back to the room on the gurney.

I was informed the next day they found nothing wrong with my kidney—our prayers were answered. I was released from the hospital—can't say I was impressed with socialized medicine.

Chapter VI

The Long Walk

Terry began making preparations for his walk into the interior of Suriname: quite extensive preparations. He planned on a three-week trip with a week to rest before returning to work. Kelly, a pilot he knew, would fly him to Sipaliwinni, the southernmost airport in Suriname—there, three guides from the Trio Indian village of Alalapadu were scheduled to meet him.

From Sipaliwinni, the route turned southeast to Pousoe Tirio, Brazil, bordering Suriname. Then, after spending a couple of days there, it was west to Alalapadu. New guides would await him there to continue on to the headwaters of the Tapanahoni River where he'd be met by the canoe from the geological department of Suralco. The canoe was scheduled to take him downriver where the Paloemeu River joined the Tapanahoni River. From there, Kelly was to fly him back to Paramaribo.

Terry sought advice from a variety of sources: Peter Bolwerk, Suriname Museum, Neil Bittle, Missionary Aviation Fellowship; H. Coutinho and J. Malm, Suralco Geological Department; J. Janssen, Suralco Moengo Mine; M. Rambharos, Leledorp Mine; L. MacArthur, Suralco Paranam Operations; Father Donicie, Catholic Missionary Headquarters in Paramaribo; and Claude Leavitt, Foreign Language Institute at Alalapadu.

Our son Kevin and I accompanied Terry when he talked to Father Donicie. He was Dutch and had spent most of his thirty-five years as a priest in Suriname. He worked with U.S. servicemen here in WWII and knew English and the American way of doing things. He was known and respected by the Indians and the Bush Negroes as well as the people in the city: if he didn't have the answer, he knew who did—a prime source of sound information.

While we were there, Father Waldie Wong Loi Sing, the newly ordained

Surinamer priest, came into the room. Terry had just asked Father Donicie for his blessing on the trip: Father said Father Waldie's blessing would have all that new innocence and was better; in the end, both gave him their blessing.

Conferring with all these people, Terry learned what type of food to carry, what first aid items were needed, what type of snake-bite kit to get and what type of utensils were necessary.

To carry all the supplies, he needed a *motete*: a local version of the packboard. It's a basket woven by the Indians and Bush Negroes: three sides, rectangular in shape, with the top open, straps for the arms and one for the head. When in use, that strap was placed on the forehead which naturally brought the head in a lowered position to help hold the weight of the *moetete*.

Larry MacArthur obtained one the day before Terry's scheduled departure; Larry and his eighty-year old full-blooded Indian grandmother showed Terry how to pack it, cover it with a large piece of plastic and then lace the open side together with a nylon line making the motete compact and watertight.

That evening, we all went to the 7:00 p.m. Mass. Sunday morning, August 2, 1970, Terry Sr., Terry Jr. and Kevin took off from Zorg en Hoop airport with Ed Kelly piloting the 182. Their destination: Sipaliwini airport about twenty kilometers north of the border with Brazil, a two-hour-and-fifty-five-minute flight; there, three Trio Indian guides were scheduled to meet him.

About noon, Binto, a young man from Zorg en Hoop airport, stopped by the house to tell us Terry radioed them: He and the boys were on the ground in Sipaliwini—Kelly and the boys would be taking off shortly for the return trip.

I waited until about three in the afternoon before going to the airport to pick them up: the 182 was just coming into view as I drove in.

"Were the guides there when you arrived?"

"We didn't see them anywhere when we landed—then Dad noticed some movement on the far side of the field as we unloaded the plane. The three guides had been sitting there, shading themselves with a type of broad leaf—like a banana leaf; no one at the tower were aware of their presence."

"They left the village of Alalapadu on Thursday—it took them three days to walk to the airport—Dad's going to have a lot of walking to do."

The boys were also amazed at the size of the strip at the airport in Sipaliwini: vas part of a project called Operation Grasshopper intended to help open up the interior. The strip was large enough to accommodate a DC 3-type aircraft. The tower was mounted on top of the radio and flight room; another small building held the generating plant and several other buildings housed the personnel and supplies.

Now we wait—the canoe from the geological department of Suralco was scheduled to meet Terry at the headwaters of the Tapanahoni River three weeks from today. The Missionary Air Fellowship group in Paramaribo was in radio contact with Claude Leavitt and his family living in Alalapadu: our first contact point with Terry after his visit to Pousoe Tirio in Brazil.

On the fourth of August, Larry MacArthur, one of Terry's trainees, driving Terry's work truck M188, came into our driveway. All the kids automatically yelled "Daddy, Daddy, Daddy." Larry about died laughing—he brought mail from Terry's box at work and asked if I needed anything.

During the days that followed, neighbors and friends quite often asked if we heard from Terry—answering in the negative, I explained I didn't expect to hear anything until the eleventh or twelfth.

Rambharos, another of Terry's trainees, a surveyor for the government before working for Suralco, knew what walking in the jungle was like—he was concerned.

"Don't worry, Mrs. McCarthy, I'll take care of you and the children and help you get back to the States."

"Thank you, Rambharos, but I know Terry's alright."

Larry MacArthur also knew the jungle quite well and was not concerned.

"I know your husband well enough to tell you he'll come back one way or another."

"Thanks, Larry, I know that too."

On the morning of August 13, I received a phone call from the MAF headquarters in Paramaribo.

"Mrs. McCarthy, this is Claude Leavitt—I'm in the city right now but there is a gentleman with three of our Trio Indians who arrived in Alalapadu this morning—we've been in radio contact with him and he wants to talk to you."

"Wow, that's great news—I'll be right over."

It was wonderful talking to Terry on the radio.

"We're a day late but we're okay."

"It's just good to hear your voice."

"Would you go to the geological department and give them some more money—I'll need it to pay the crew coming upriver to pick me up."

"Okay, I'll do that."

"I won't spend as much time here as I planned because we were a day late arriving here—Claude is doing fine work here in writing the language of the Trio Indians. There is so much to see. The clinic staffed by Dutch missionaries is well stocked. The Missionary Air Fellowship has a landing field here—they actually flew in parts of the wooden clinic building in their little plane until the building was complete."

"That pilot we know, Neil Bittle, probably did all of that, didn't he?"

"Yes, he did—they are fine people."

"Will you still come home on schedule?"

"Yes. The geological department's schedule for meeting me can't be changed so I'll see you on the twenty-third. It'll be all river transportation after we meet them at the Tapanahoni River."

"We'll be waiting for you—keep safe."

On Sunday, August 23, we were at Zorg en Hoop airport when the 182 landed with Kelly, Terry, Rory, Bob (the latter two accompanied Kelly to Paloemeu), the *motete*, a little green parrot, Frankie, who hitched a ride downriver with Terry, and two sets of beautiful bows and arrows.

Terry, quite a few pounds lighter, walked to us, his head bent forward as though he still had the strap of his motete on his forehead. Camille was the first to speak.

"Daddy, you smell from smoke."

"I know I do—the Indians and I cooked with a wood fire for three weeks: I've traveled to a different world and back again."

At home, it was difficult for him to settle down with all the children asking questions at once. First things first, though, a long shower was in order and the smoky clothes put in the washer. Then Dad unpacked all the goodies and had a "show and tell."

With Frankie sitting on his perch, Terry brought out his other treasures. A small container (made from skin) with poison tips (soaked in curare), a small an headdress made up of the very small yellow and red face feathers of the multi-colored macaw; a beautiful bead belt; a small basket-woven pouch; a pair of carved combs; a basket-woven cassava squeezer, three flutes, a pair of anteater claws, a pair of Indian nose feathers, one set of Indian arm feathers and the two bows and seven arrows.

The green parrot, Frankie, was too young to fend for himself so we fed him milk-soaked cassava bread—that's what he was fed on the trip downriver—what an appetite he had. Flint wasn't too happy with all the attention given to Frankie and let us know about it, loud and clear.

The Indians told Terry to just keep Frankie's wing feathers clipped and it wouldn't be necessary to cage him. His perch was on the back patio during the day. However, we apparently didn't clip his feathers enough. One day, as I sat with him on the patio, he flew away and never returned.

In the days that followed, Terry discovered some extra problems with his feet. He went to Dr. Brocksma to check them out. He showed Terry a book that explained he had some parasites in his foot sores—little bugs that live on dogs had somehow gotten into the open sores on his feet: no known cure. These bugs tunnel under the skin and look for a home but they cannot live in humans. They continue to burrow but, not finding a home, they die.

The doctor recommended the use of a freeze spray. Wherever the critters traveled, the skin was upset and turned somewhat red—it looked like the tunnel of a ground mole. By freeze spraying the area ahead of the tunnel, some of them were killed. All of them finally died off and Terry's feet again looked normal.

All the rolls of film from the trip were developed into slides—the managing director of Suralco, Waldo Porter, was interested in seeing them. What a terrific show unfolded as Mr. Porter, his wife, and our family watched and traveled with Terry and the guides through the jungle. He made it to the Brazilian border and visited the Catholic mission there, then back into Suriname to the village of Alalapadu where Claude Leavitt lived. The camp sites from there to the Tapanahoni River were routine. The Suralco boat met him there and took him downriver to Palamoeu—he radioed Zorg-en-Hoop Airport from there and Kelly picked him up the next morning and brought him home: quite an undertaking!

Now, we entered another phase of our life. At the end of August, we made reservations for dinner for the family at the Tororica Hotel downtown: the occasion—Terry Jr. was leaving to start his college work in the States. This was our last function as a family unit per se here in Suriname.

September 4 he was on his way—I'll never forget how I felt as I saw him walk up the stairs of the airplane—if I hadn't been leaning on Terry, I think my legs would have given out. It was difficult knowing he was on his way to another country. I remembered him leaving home on his first day of school as a little boy: it's not that you love the first one more—the first one always starts a new phase of life for the family and it needs "getting used to."

The empty place at the table that evening spoke loudly as the hush fell on those gathered. He wasn't there in the van either, picking me up as I finished shopping downtown later in the week. I made more trips to the Suralco office than usual to pick up the mail, hoping there was a letter today. The clerk, who changed dollars into guilders for me at the office, said she could always tell when I found a letter from Terry in the box—my smile was brighter.

For me, the children leaving was the hardest phase of our life—I guess being in a foreign country probably made it more difficult. I knew each year another one would leave—we'd be so far apart.

Firsthand news about Terry Jr. came a little later. Suralco had Jack Snead from the fire fighting training part of Texas A&M Extension Service come down to Suriname to do some training. Jack knew Terry Jr. was at A&M at the time and visited him before coming. Jack had dinner with us one night during his stay.

"Thecla, I visited Terry last week."

"Great, how is he doing?"

"Well, he's okay. Actually, when I saw him, he was sitting at the table studying—I hate to tell you this—he had an ice bag on his forehead."

"An ice bag—what for?"

"He's on the scrub team practicing with the regular football team—his forehead is sort of black and blue where the helmet guard is. I don't think the helmet fits too well. But he's okay."

"Thanks, Jack, for visiting him—I guess some people really like football. Give him my love when you see him again."

So life goes on.

My River

Restless river many faces you display
in the passing of one day.
You chatter and ripple
in the early morning sun
your face shows dimples
and your bustling's for fun.

But the day moves on,
toward the sea you should flow,
but, too close to the sea you reside
and with it are ruled by the tide.
You push hard, the tide equally as well
as higher and higher you swell
then exquisite calm—your face lays bare.

Today, I feel a struggle inside:
anger, hurt surge up;
love, patience equally abide
neither relenting, higher and higher they swell
but where can I find peace, my fears to quell?

The tide has called back, your struggle won
you slowly drop and glide smoothly on.
my hope drops with you and in creeps despair
let me enfold myself in your arms
free to glide along, my heart laid bare
on and on to the sea, away from all harm.

Forgive me, river, I've not listened well
you accept the Creator's plan—there peace dwells.
Each day you struggle the tide
never relenting, you never hide.
That's why you play in the morning sun
and your calm reflects trees when day's done.
Now my struggle for today is won;
I'll take the rest as you do, one by one.

Chapter VII

Paranam—The Paranam Works

One of the indigenous wooden houses in Paranam became available. We put in our request for it—it was granted: our family moved to our new home. The village of Paranam received its name for its location where the Para River met the Suriname River.

The house, situated in a little neighborhood around the staff club, was near the mine; that made it much more convenient for Terry. The older boys lived near our home now too—they still used one of the nearby trailers as their bedrooms and school rooms but they shared meals with us again.

It was a very large house, built on high stilts, overlooking the Suriname River, a short distance from the docks of the Paranam Works. The back entrance opened into a small hall between the kitchen and the maid's room and bathroom. (The maid's room was our bedroom.) Beyond the kitchen was the dining room separated by an arch into the living room. A long narrow room, one side of which had many windows overlooking the river, was open to both the dining room and living room. This was our music room—no piano, just our stereo with all the records. (When Americans from the ships at the dock walked by on the road on their way to the staff club, they always stopped in surprise when they heard the State-side records.)

The front door opened into a hall separating the living room on the left from the three large bedrooms and two bathrooms on the right. The hardwood floors added to the beauty of the house. The breeze from the river kept the house cool inside all through the day.

Shortly after we moved in, a man came to the back door.

"I'm looking for Mr. DeFarria."

"He lives in the house next door, sir."

"Thank you."

I heard a knock on the front door a few minutes later—there stood the same man with a startled look on his face.

"This is our front door, sir—De Farrias live in that house over there."

"This whole house is yours?"

"Yes, sir, it is."

He shook his head as he walked away.

The ample space under the house, because of the stilts, held a closed laundry room at one end. Terry's company truck was parked alongside of that. A small cement patio with chairs and plants added color to the middle of the area. The PA 18 plane, wings tied above it in the rafters, stood forlornly, stripped of its fabric, on the side of the patio. Clotheslines graced the area to the right of that. The VW bus was garaged under the children's bedrooms, the VW bug under our bedroom.

Usually, a bunch of bananas hung somewhere under the house—Keith DeFarria, one of the Surinamer friends of the boys, kept us supplied with them. He tasted a banana cream pie I made one day—he said if I made one for his birthday, he'd keep me supplied with bananas. I baked that pie for his birthday—his mother told me later that he ate the entire pie himself.

Keith, known to us as Keetsha, had a voice and laughter that could wake the dead—you always knew when he arrived home from school. He called out as he passed our house on his *bromfiets* (a motorized bicycle).

One Sunday afternoon we heard his call from the river—a boat carrying him and several other men was coming to shore. When the boat was tied up, we saw the cause of all the excitement—they were carrying a tiger up to their house.

"We hunted upriver in the jungle and saw nothing; then coming downstream in the boat, we saw this tiger swimming across the river and shot him."

We were quite impressed with their trophy—Keetsha gave Terry one of the big teeth as a remembrance.

My efforts to keep chairs, potted plants and flowers on the cement patio below the house (a pleasant spot that caught the breeze from the river) were often thwarted by the necessity to use the cement floor of the patio to repair and maintain our vehicles. It seemed the boys, under the supervision of Terry, always had something apart—the cement pad was needed for that type of work. Despite this, I did spend quite a few afternoons during our stay in my favorite spot.

From the patio, a sidewalk extended through the center of the large front lawn to the road. The river was a short distance beyond the road. Across the river, the unbroken jungle spread out as far as the eye could see.

The river was ruled by the ocean—as the tide came in, the river rose. When it reached its peak, it was perfectly calm for a time and reflected the trees of the jungle on the other side. In the quiet of the late afternoon, the call of the monkeys in the jungle could be heard.

Late Afternoon

That time before sunset
when the world is hushed
a moment when all is still.
The river holds the jungle's
reflection—so perfectly
framed by the elegant palm,
a painting hung in earth's gallery
eternal, untouched beauty.

Silent wall of tree and vine
do you look at us and see
trees cut to fashion houses,
their absence marked by
trimmed lawns, enclosed gardens
of flowers and rows of orange trees?

Do the eyes of creatures you house
look with you at our temporal beauty
and in your hearts rejoice
that you are as yet untamed?

The moment passes.
The evening breeze caresses
the face of the river
sending the reflection scattering,

ruffles the fronds of the palm,
brushes by my face to
bring the fragrance of
orange trees in blossom as
compensation for disturbing
the stillness and bringing back reality.

The ships that were loaded at the Paranam docks came upstream in front of our house to a wider section of the river a short distance away: there they let the current of the outgoing tide turn them around and take them back downriver to the ocean. It was startling to see them when you looked out the window—they appeared huge as they moved silently by with only the jungle as a backdrop.

The younger children rode the bus to school in Paramaribo every day while the older boys studied in their trailer. Late afternoons and weekends were spent in all kinds of adventure. Sometimes, playing the part of marines, the children, led by Chris, went through the marshy jungle a short distance beyond our neighborhood to fight a battle. When the troop returned one afternoon, they could hardly wait to tell me about their adventure.

"Mom, we were sloshing through the jungle and Chris shouted Retreat!"

"Yeah, as we turned we saw a small green boa hanging from a tree, staring at Chris."

"We came back in a hurry."

I received a call that afternoon from a distraught mother of a family who recently arrived from the States.

"How in the world do you get that awful musty smell out of your boys' clothes after they've been in the jungle?"

"I have them hose down their clothes in the driveway when they come home, then put them in the washer—it helps."

Brigid still shudders when she thinks about the boa constrictor Dad brought home in the bed of his pickup one day—thirteen feet long, it was securely fastened to the truck.

The snake was found in the mine by a worker who wanted Dad to see it. From there it made the rounds to the office and other sections of the mine for display and then to our home.

One of the workers, a Carib Indian, said he'd like to have it—he coiled it up, put it in bag and took it home.

Some afternoons, the boys went to the mine equipment boneyard to look for pieces of scrap to construct something.

One such undertaking produced a go-cart: it sported a lawn mower motor mounted on a board behind the seat of the cart: the motor stood upright so the spark plug was sticking out on top of the motor. The transmission came from some sort of power table saw. It had a lever for forward or reverse motion. On the first try, Cronan's body didn't accelerate as fast as the forward speed of the cart: he ended up sitting atop the spark plug: that evoked a yell as the spark plug shocked him.

They roared around the house and pathways in the neighborhood. It had no tail pipe or muffler: everyone knew when and where the go-cart was running.

The transmission they used had a hydraulic pump which Cronan found was the same as those used in the jet engines he works on today.

Then, Leishe, the Tibetan terrier, came back into our lives as unexpectedly as the first time. As noted in an earlier chapter, she came at that time on a temporary basis and returned to the Serdaley family when the mother and children arrived in Suriname.

Soon after Leishe left us, Flint the macaw was added to our family. He ruled from his perch and raised a ruckus if anything displeased him.

Laurel Serdaley called one day.

"Steve is finished with his work for World Health here—he's being transferred to Washington, D.C. The complex where we'll live there doesn't allow dogs, so would you take Leishe?"

"Yes, of course I will."

"Thanks so much, I'm glad she'll have a good home. We'll bring her to you soon."

When Leishe arrived, Flint took one look at her and objected in his loudest voice. He tried in every way to get down to the floor from his perch. Leishe turned around and headed for the door—they were never reconciled. What a combination of pets these two were: a dog terrified of a bird and a bird who thought that was really cool.

One day, I put a big ham bone in Leishe's dish in the back hall by the door. She went to the dish and started chewing on it. At the same time, Sean took Flint off his perch and placed him on the floor—Flint marched to the hall (he always marched rather than walked). Leishe saw him coming and ran into our bedroom; Flint picked up the bone in his beak and paraded around showing it off to Leishe. He looked so funny with the big bone in his beak.

So I spent some time with Flint and some with Leishe. I have a couple of scars on my right hand from Flint—I carried him around at times; when he saw someone he disliked approaching us, he became so irritated he bit me because he couldn't get at them. Then he'd look so sorry and try to lick the spot on my hand. Sometimes I took him with me when I drove the van—he perched on the back of the seat beside me. No stranger could come near the open window of the van when I was parked—he was very protective of me.

Jane loved Leishe. In the morning, I took her with me when I went to the village to pick up Jane at the bus stop. Leishe could be at the farther end of the house when I quietly took the keys to the car off the hook in the hall by the back door. She came skittering around the corner from the bedrooms through the living room, dining room and kitchen to the back hall and waited for the door to open.

In the village, we passed a house where several dogs lived—they had a fit barking when they saw Leishe looking out the window. After a few days of this, she began watching how many times I shifted the car before coming to that house—one day she lay down in the seat, jumped up at that house and got the first bark at the dogs. That really pleased her. She always sat on Jane's lap on the way home and followed her everywhere as she cleaned the house— Flint was on his perch during that time so he couldn't harass them.

Jane knew Flint slept under Sean's bed at night—Bob, who liked teasing Jane, sometimes lay under Sean's bed as he heard Jane arrive. When she came into the bedroom to clean, Bob grabbed her toes as she came near the bed.

"Mommy, Mommy, bad boy Bob," was heard as she chased him down the hall with the broom.

The Creoles really celebrate their fortieth birthday—when Jane turned forty, she asked me to take a picture of her holding Leishe. She invited our family to her house for cake. The house was built about a foot off the ground because sometimes the river flooded into that area. When we arrived, the younger children and I started going inside—the floor began to creak. Jane ran to the door before the older boys could come in.

"Boys, boys, I bring cake outside—you break house."

"Okay, Jane. We don't want to break your floors."

The boys had a good laugh over that—they still do when they get together and talk about it.

Jane and Leishe

One day I received a letter from Laurel Serdaley—there was a Tibetan Terrier Club where they now lived. She wanted Leishe back so she could be bred—she said I could have one of her puppies.

I dreaded sending her to the States—she was attached to the family and I remembered how frightened she was from her original trip to Suriname. There was nothing I could do about it—I didn't own her.

I took her to the veterinarian to be checked and get the tranquilizers needed for the trip. Her flight left Zanderij Airport at 4:30 a.m.—Terry and I left home at 3:00. I had given Leishe the tranquilizer and expected her to fall asleep in my lap; instead she sat there and looked at me the whole trip to the airport. When she heard the whine of the jet engines, she went wild—we forced her into her carrier, handed her to the man at the counter along with the food for the trip and returned home.

Laurel wrote that Leishe arrived but had bitten anyone who tried to give her food and water along the way back. I didn't correspond with her anymore even when she later wrote asking if I preferred a male or female puppy of Leishe.

Jane really missed Leishe—she couldn't believe that Laurel wanted her back.

One big event in the lives of the children was the addition of a dugout canoe to the family. Bob wrote about this.

Robert

I remember how excited I was when Dad told us that Larry MacArthur, one of the men he was training, had purchased a canoe in Moengo for us. It was to be shipped to Paranam via one of the regular ore barges.

Not long after Dad's announcement, a beautiful dugout appeared in the mouth of the canal that was just outside of the plant gate in the town of Paranam where Mom went to pick up Jane Holder. We were sure that was our canoe. We were sure that it had somehow not gotten delivered to us.

Finally, however, after we had given up on it, our real canoe showed up. I don't remember the details of the delivery but our excitement soon turned to disappointment when the half-inch-wide crack in the lower hull was taking forever to get repaired. It sat upside down on two sawhorses beneath the house for another eternity.

Finally, one day a carpenter showed up with his tool box. We crowded in around him asking a million questions. All he would say as he sounded the hull with his hammer and hitched up his pants was, "You see how I gonna fix it!" It seems to me that he pondered his actions for days while he sounded with his hammer and hitched up his pants with his forearms.

Eventually, he began to cut out the split section of the hull. The solid wooden hull had apparently not tolerated its exposure to the sun on the ride over from Moengo on top of the barge. Such a dugout canoe seldom leaves the water after it is hewn from a solid tree trunk. It remains immersed in water where the wood will not split. To us, it seemed a huge hole that he was sawing as he continued to answer a million questions with, "You see how I gonna fix it!"

He sawed at an angle which gave the hole an outward bevel. In other words, the hole was wider on the outside of the hull. I seem to remember that the hole was about five inches wide by about a foot and a half long. He then fashioned a patch to fit into the hole. The bevel on the edge of the patch matched that of the hole. In that way, the water pressure from the hull's displacement increased the pressure on the calk that he used on the patch

The patch was calked and fit into place. We helped hold the patch in place while he attached the two cross pieces on the inside of the hull which held it in place. Finally, with a few final raps of his hammer along the hull and hitching his pants once more, he called it finished, picked up his tools and left.

She was ready to launch. We were certainly proud of our canoe! It had a used look with dull coloring on her gunwales. She turned up bow and stern to high points which had some shallow carving in them. She was about fifteen or sixteen feet stem to stern. Just forward of the turned-up stern, a hole had been sawn out of the hull for a motor. A bulkhead of solid inch-and-a-half-thick wood had been installed forward of the hole which served as a transom for mounting the motor.

I don't remember how we launched her. She must have weighed over 300 pounds. In a land of so much water, portaging is not necessary. It was not long though, before she became part of life in Paranam. For us, it was our first experience in a canoe—a 300-pound round-bottomed dugout. Our training program involved frequent wet clothes. Long before we ever knew what it was called, the paddle J-stroke became a part of life. In a river with two currents, a 300-pound canoe could go wherever we wanted it to. It was only a matter of going with the tidal flows.

A nearby creek which was narrow but very deep became a wonderful adventure at high tide. We would have to dip the bow underneath fallen trees and each of us would step over the fallen trunk in turn. We could work our way up the creek as far as possible then ride the current of the receding tide back out. That is how we soon had the tip of the bow broken off. The tip was unable to withstand striking a low-lying tree trunk with the combined momentum of the out-flowing water, the massive hull and the weight of the occupants. Despite our desperate back-paddling, it took that tip off in a snap.

One day on an adventure up that creek, a beady-eyed snake of unknown variety lay in a coil on top of the tree trunk blocking the way. I had passed the bow under the trunk as usual and was preparing to climb over it when I noticed the snake. I decided to be rid of it by whacking it with my paddle. It was quite upset when it landed between my feet in the bottom of the canoe. We managed to keep the canoe upright, but it got quite exciting before we were able to send the snake on its way.

One day the canoe disappeared. We never found out whether it was taken away by the tide or by someone. When I get the chance, I'll tell some of the adventures we had like the broad elephant-like back of the manatee which briefly surfaced beside us out of the muddy murk of the river, about the ghost mine Rorak, about the Barge, the ghost plantation and Dad's paddle.

Thanks, Mom and Dad! There has never been a classroom like that one.

Cronan found later in life, when learning to fly, that the same type of maneuver was needed when landing an airplane in a cross wind as they learned when maneuvering the canoe across the current of the river in Suriname.

One particular Sunday morning after Mass, when we still had the canoe, Rory took Chris, Bob, Cronan and a neighbor, Bert Screen, out on the river in the canoe. Ruled by the tide, it rises about fourteen feet when the tide is in— is very calm and smooth until the tide goes out again. Then the current is very swift. The tide was going out as they were bringing the canoe into shore—a couple of barges were anchored upstream from the Paranam docks: Rory knew the swift current would suck the canoe under the first barge before they reached shore.

"Everyone, jump into the river and swim to shore."

They obeyed him: into the river they went; Rory swam to the front of the barge and held on there—Chris had just started swimming lessons at the pool: he didn't like jumping into the water but followed Rory's command. Rory saw he was having difficulty.

"Chris, just float down to me and I'll catch you."

Rory had anchored himself to the outer edge of the barge—Chris did as he was told: Rory caught him in his arms—he held on so tight, Rory could hardly breathe. They watched the canoe go under the barge, pop up on the other side, then under the next barge.

It was recovered and returned by workmen at the Paranam docks. Rory still had an ashen look when he came into the house that morning and still has some recurring nightmares about it—thank heaven for guardian angels.

Rambharos invited our family to spend a weekend with his family at a beach in the Coronie District on the northern shore of Suriname. Cronan wrote about it later and gives a good description of it.

Cronan

My family and I took an excursion across the northern part of the country. The trip was over a weekend and we spent the night at a beach. We started early on Saturday morning and drove from Paranam into Paramaribo, where we met our friend Rambharos. Up to now, the trip was quite uneventful since it was only thirty miles on a paved highway with a bike path alongside it.

We left Paramaribo and headed west across the northern side of Suriname. We rode a ferry across the Wayambo River; then crossed Piruvia Kreek on a small ferry guided by a cable.

After these crossings, things took a turn for the worse. The road was no longer paved—actually, it really wasn't a road. The pot holes were so big, you'd lose sight of the car ahead—good thing is was the dry season. Dad drove very cautiously at first over the washboard bumps since we had a VW van— that soon changed as we lost sight of the other car. To catch up, we had to drive fast and found that was the better way to go—just "fly" over the bumps. I don't know how that van survived.

That night we camped on the beach. Now, this is the first time I saw a beach in Suriname. I had these vivid pictures of Samara, Costa Rica—a five-mile-long white sand beach in a natural bay that was protected from the open ocean by a reef. The beach in Suriname was not that! It is built of the silt dropped by the Amazon River in Brazil. In other words, it's all mud!

For the night, we spread blankets on the little grass along the edge of the beach—the smaller kids slept inside the van. Lying on the beach, the wind was quite brisk. I slipped back to find a corner to sleep inside the van or just lie downwind of the van for a wind break—I chose the latter. That was a wrong move—mosquitos! They had the same idea and back out into the wind I went.

The next morning I woke to find the sun up and decided to go for a walk with my brothers in the mu - oops, I mean the beach. Curious-looking things covered the beach. As the waves came in, these "things" would move along with the flow but out of the water, they just lay there not moving. It turned out to be rolls of clay: the waves rolled them around and they would get more and more clay built up until they were all about four inches long and one inch around.

That day was a Sunday so, as usual, we went to find a Catholic church in the area—we found one. It had a dusty, gravel parking lot and several large trees for shade. The whole family went in except our parrot, Flint. He stayed perched on the back of the last seat in the van. It wasn't hard for him to hang on to the seat since the wild trip out here had his claw marks embedded into it permanently.

As in all churches, everyone joins in the singing of hymns. My family and I arrived early and found a pew in the middle of the church. The Mass began with a song as the priest entered. When the singing began, an awful sound, like someone making fun of our singing, came from outside: "Ahhhh," in a monotone went on and on throughout the song. Nobody but our family even noticed it. My brothers and I were about to fall on the floor laughing. Mom didn't think it was funny though: she kept motioning to us to stop our giggling. How could we—we knew it was Flint. He was trying to outdo our singing with his own singing just like he always did at home when we sang. That was only the first song—do you know how many songs there are during Mass?

After Mass, we went back to the beach and joined Rambharos and family for lunch and then began our long return trip.

A year or so later, Dad took Bob and me on a cross-country training flight in his 182. The first leg of the flight was over the road to Coronie—we could see the bumps on the road from up there!

Jane Sharkey, daughter of the smelter supervisor, lived near us in Paramaribo when we first arrived in Suriname—she spent a lot of time at our house then. We didn't see much of her after we moved to Paranam but we learned Jane returned to the States for college—we bought the Honda 50 motorbike she left behind.

The bike needed repairs; the boys ordered bearings and a chain for it from the States: the bike lay idle for a long time awaiting the parts. When they finally arrived, they were installed: the Honda was their favorite mode of transportation after that.

One afternoon, I asked the boys if I could try out their motorbike—we did some practice runs near the house and then I took off on the roads around the little housing area—it was fun.

A few days later, I made my usual rounds on it: as I approached the turn onto the road to our house, the front wheel hit some loose gravel on the side of the road—instead of the brake, I pushed the accelerator: off I went into the drainage ditch. The bike stayed there but I found myself among the bushes on the other side. I saw a few stars and felt a little blood trickle by my left eye. The children saw it happen and came running over.

"Is she dead?" I heard Hilary cry.

I looked up at their faces and said: "I'm so sorry I ruined your bike—you'll probably have to buy another chain..."

"Mom, the bike is okay—it's you we're worried about."

I walked away from that one and decided to quit while I was still ahead.

A little later, when I attended a coffee for the expatriates' wives at the home of the new superintendent's wife, I received a lecture from her. We American wives don't do things like riding a motorbike—that is not setting a good example for the local people; being injured made it worse. Working for a large company was a lot different than having our own contract.

I always tried using the local foods to cook—I relied on Jane to teach me how to cook them. One day our menu included a new and odd entrée—an iguana filled with eggs. Rory shot it with a pellet gun down by the river and brought it home for us to see: Jane was elated.

"Rory, you take skin off—I show Mommy how to cook it."

Rory worked hard to get the skin off: Jane dressed it and was particularly delighted with the amount of eggs in it. She boiled the eggs and I fried the other parts with curry as she instructed me—the fried parts were very tasty; the eggs Jane took home with her. Rory tried one egg—the shell was hard to get off and the inside not too enjoyable.

Another time, Terry brought home a cayman tail someone at the mine gave him—it was extracted from the outer skin. Once again, Jane came to the rescue and taught me how to cook it.

We frequently saw cayman on the highway between Paramaribo and Paranam—they lived in the large drainage ditches beside the road. They are crocodilian but looked more like an alligator. They have free run of the highway. Terry encountered one about five feet long one day: he came snapping across the highway ready to do battle with the truck.

Getting to Mass on Sundays was not too difficult. We still went to an English Mass in Paramaribo once a month—the other Sundays we went to the local churches where the Dutch language was used. The Liturgy of the Mass is the same everywhere in the world.

The church in the little village of Paranam was located on the other side of the Paranam docks from our house. If a ship had recently been loaded with alumina (the name given to pure aluminum-oxide) at the dock, the church and the village were bathed in what looked like a dusting of snow. Alumina is white in color with the texture of fine salt and is blown into the hold of the ship: naturally, some of it escapes. When that happened, the benches and the altar in the church were coated with the powder. They were cleaned before Mass was celebrated but it was still noticeable.

On Palm Sunday, the parishioners really celebrate the commemoration of Jesus' triumphal entry into Jerusalem. Outside the church, holding our palm branches, we sang and danced to the song in the local Taki-Taki language and rhythm—*"a la palma, palma, me de go."*

If a priest was not available in Paranam for Mass, we went to a parish a few miles distant in Copieweg—a school was attached to the parish there. The parish supported itself with a chicken farm which was housed very near the church. The aroma of chickens permeated the "tropical style" church with its many open spaces. Birds made their nests near the altar—they flew in and out feeding their young during Mass. Some dogs also came in to lie on the cool cement floor.

I am reminded of the church in Copieweg each time we now pray Psalm 84 on Monday, week III of our Liturgy of the Hours: "the sparrow herself finds a home and the swallow a nest for her brood; she lays her young by your altars, Lord of hosts, my king and my God."

One particular Sunday, on the way home from Copieweg, we stopped as usual before crossing the mine haul road near Paranam. There we noticed a sloth moving as best it could alongside the road—its legs certainly not conducive to walking on the ground. What was it doing here with no trees, their usual habitat, in sight? We had to check that out.

Cronan picked it up; it slowly turned its head to get a good look at the intruder—the expression on that cute little face seemed to say, "Now, why did you do that?"

Legs sprawled, he slowly tried to wriggle from Cronan's hand. No success in that, it calmly turned his head around to get a look at all of us as it was placed in the van—it seemed capable of actually swiveling its head.

At home, Cronan placed it on the trunk of a nearby tree; it v e r y s l o w l y c l i m b e d u p t o t h e f i r s t a v a i l a b l e b r a n c h, hung upside down for a while, turned its head almost completely around to get a last look at us and c o n t i n u e d u p t o t h e t o p o f t h e t r e e.

Cronan holding sloth

Father Joop Calis, OMI, a missionary priest from Holland, offered the English Mass at times at the Catholic Center in Paramaribo. He was a big strong man with a full beard. Most of his time was spent at various Missions in the interior—Indian and Bush Negro parishes. His headquarters, PAS was in Paramaribo; at times we visited with him and the lay missionaries who worked with him. Pet monkeys and all sorts of animals filled their yard.

On one of these occasions, Terry told him our family was in need of a retreat.

"Father, would you consider spending a weekend in Paranam to give us a retreat?"

"You asked me this at just the right time—I need some time off where it's quiet."

"Great, you tell me when and I'll request a trailer for you to stay in—we'll have the retreat and all the meals at our house."

A date was set: Father came out early on a Friday evening, gave us a little talk and ended with night prayers and retired to his trailer. Early the next morning, he offered Mass for us at the dining room table and exposed the Blessed Sacrament on the buffet which was decorated with flowers and candles. He reposed the Blessed Sacrament at Benediction in the evening.

His talks were given as we gathered in the living room. Most of the meals were prepared in advance so it was a matter of warming the food at mealtime.

He was a good retreat master—we learned much about our Faith from him as well as his experiences in his missionary work. In Africa, at the time of the Mau Mau uprising, he barely escaped with his life. In his work with the Bush Negroes in Suriname, he witnessed their rituals and pointed out some mistakes they were making—he saw those rituals firsthand in Africa.

In one of the Indian villages here in Suriname where Father offered Mass, there was a little girl exceptionally strong in her Faith. She contracted a fever and was dying—he was called to give her the Sacrament of the Sick which can heal or prepare one for dying. He was with her when she died: a white dove flew into the sky as she drew her last breath—the only white dove he had ever seen there.

Nothing deterred him from spreading the Good News. He needed access to remote villages. When he was still in Africa, he talked a man he knew in Holland into buying a small plane for him—then he had to learn to fly.

Now he had a push-pull plane, a Cessna Skymaster—PAS built a hanger for it at Zorg-en-Hoop airport. This type of plane was best for short runways. The villagers built the airstrips—he gave them the dimensions: they cleared the land with their tools. At the airport, a loud roar always announced his take-offs and landings. He said the last item on his take-off checklist was the Act of Contrition.

Terry rented a space in the PAS hanger when he later brought the Cessna 182 down. That enabled him to completely strip down and repaint the plane in a closed area—the cost for rent: $25 a month.

Terry met Neil Bittle, the pilot for the Missionary Air Fellowship one day at the airport. We hadn't seen much of him and his wife, Meridi after we moved to Paranam.

"How's everything going, Neil?"

"We've had quite a few flights out to the missions lately—I'm a little stressed out right now."

"There are some trailers vacant in Paranam—how would you like to spend a weekend out there? It's nice and quiet and you'd have access to the swimming pool too."

"I think that would be perfect. My wife was wondering where we could go to get away from it all for a few days. I'll get back with you."

We knew Meridi was the radio contact for all the flights between Paramaribo and the various missions. We saw them occasionally at gatherings of American families in Paramaribo. She and Neil were accomplished musicians—at a Christmas party we attended, he accompanied her on the piano as she sang "Oh, Holy Night." It was beautiful.

She also had some interesting stories to tell about some of Neil's flights. One time, an Indian woman was having a very difficult time trying to deliver her baby. The nurse at the clinic wanted Neil to fly the woman to the hospital in Paramaribo. The woman and her mother got on the plane. As they gained altitude, the change in pressure brought on the contractions and the mother delivered the baby on board. Grandmother, mother and baby were doing well when they arrived in Paramaribo—so was Neil.

We were so pleased that we could offer them a little respite now. Neil, Meridi and their baby daughter, Barbara spent a long weekend in Paranam. They really enjoyed it.

I still made my weekly trips to the rehabilitation center in Paramaribo. The volunteers there periodically got together and took holiday day trips to various places of interest. This usually included a picnic-type lunch. I was introduced to many local picnic-style dishes and added many of them to my recipe file. One was called *pom*, which was delicious served hot or cold. The basic ingredient was *papoen* (pumpkin)—it was cooked and mashed. Onions, garlic and curry powder were added to this mixture—half the mixture was placed into a baking dish. Browned chicken, flavored with garlic powder, salt and curry powder was placed on top of the mixture in the dish and the rest of the mixture placed on top of the chicken. A few dollops of butter were added on the top and the dish baked for about one and a half hours. (When we returned to the States, the cooked pumpkin was a little lighter in color but just as tasty.)

I thought a holiday trip for the patients at the center was in order now—Terry suggested a trip for them to see the Paranam Works. He talked to a foreman at the mine, Boss Paal—he was happy to make the arrangements with the company. Suralco agreed to provide bus transportation for the patients from the city to Paranam. There, they would be given a tour of the mine, the smelter and the docks.

However, when I asked to have a luncheon served at the staff club for the patients, the company refused. So we decided to have the luncheon served buffet style at our house to accommodate the thirty guests.

The patients were delighted with the invitation; on the designated day they gathered at the center where the bus picked them up. Upon arriving in Paranam, Boss Paal led the tour of the Paranam Works—they were amazed at the size of it—none of them had seen it before.

What a wonderful experience it was welcoming them into our home—first, they blessed our home and our family, sang beautiful songs and filled the house with laughter; we indeed treasured their presence.

I bought quite a few extra glasses for the occasion and have five of them left—the children still recognize them when they visit and reminisce about the wonderful time we had.

When we left Suriname in 1973, the ex-Hansen patients gave me a beautiful koebie stone pendant set in gold which the men had made—a present I treasured.

Before I close this part about the ex-Hansen patients, I must introduce you to Katy Paulsen, a dear friend who worked with me at the center. She walked into my life at a party at the home of one of the expatriates who introduced her and the love of her life, her husband Fred, as the newcomers to our group of expatriates in Villa Bella.

Her smile started in her eyes and spread over her face, catching a corner of her mouth in a special way.

"Hello, I'm Katy and I think you are Thecla—Mrs. Nevins pointed you out to me."

"Yes, I am; nice to meet you Katy."

In her sixties, she was small of stature. Her short hair was curled softly, framing her face. When she spoke there was a crisp, slight hint of New England in her voice. Her smile could melt the heart of the Merchant of Venice.

"Mrs. Nevins tells me you do some volunteer work downtown; my friend Eleanor and I would like to get involved in something like that."

"Yes, I do, Katy—I work at the rehabilitation center for ex-Hansen patients."

"Would you take us with you the next time you go?"

"Yes, I'd be glad to do that."

It was the start of a beautiful friendship. Katy, Eleanor and I became the packaging department for the work done by the women at the center. Quite often, Katy asked me to have lunch at her house on the way home from the center. We talked about writing, especially poetry—she had many of her poems published. She urged me to write.

"But my life is too hectic right now, Katy."

She didn't accept that as an excuse, and eventually I did do some writing there.

Katy loved trying out all the recipes of the local people—some turned out well, others were questionable. She invited Terry and me and another couple for dinner one evening. I went to the kitchen to offer my help. With a mischievous grin, she said: "I'm trying this local dish out on you before I make it for Fred's boss who's coming to dinner in a couple of days."

With all the seconds that were eaten she didn't need me to tell her it passed.

She also spoke at times how difficult it was for her to leave New England when Fred was transferred to Vancouver, Washington. So she immersed herself in researching the Indian tribes living in that area: some of the articles she wrote about them were published.

All too soon, Fred's work in Suriname was finished. They returned to the States and we completely lost track of each other. Years later, she learned through Alcoa that the McCarthy family was living in Arizona—on her side of the country. She and Fred came to visit us the following spring. She was still the sweet soft-spoken smiling person I had known—still busy writing.

When our son Chris moved to Portland, Oregon, his wife Gina and children, Valentin and Isabella and I always went across the Columbia River to Vancouver to see her—they loved her too. She served her home-baked cookies on her finest china for our afternoon tea.

A Tribute to My Friend, Katy

*She came into my life without
warning, quiet, soft-spoken—Katylike
Into my bustle and slightly
hectic life, dependable, lovable—Katylike
At the center packaging; crisp
fresh New Englander came—Katylike
Genteel, well-learned, flecked
with just enough Northwestern—Katylike
Luncheons in her home with talk
of writing and reading good poetry—Katylike
Too short a time—how can I let it go?
I'll keep all of it
fast in my heart—Katylike*

Katy died last November. Her son returned our Christmas letter with a note about her death. I sent him the poem I wrote about her.

Now it was time for Kevin to leave and go back to the States for college—there'd be another empty place at the table. The family didn't go to the Tororica for dinner as we did for Terry—instead Kevin took the daughter of the manager of the Paranam Works to dinner there. She was visiting her parents on her vacation break.

She met the boys at the staff club one day and volunteered to help Kevin with some of the last math lessons in the correspondence course. He usually went to her house in Paramaribo but one day, she came to Paranam instead. They decided to take a ride in the canoe after they finished the lesson—there was time to do that before she went to meet her dad for lunch at the staff club. The canoe tipped as she was getting out—she was soaked and muddy.

She took a shower at our house but didn't have any clean clothes. Brigid and Camille's clothes were too small, mine too large so she opted for a pair of the boys' jeans and a tee shirt. I took one look at her and shuddered.

"You can't go to meet your dad at the staff club in those clothes."

"Oh, he'll get over it."

Off she went. Her dad, dining with some visitors that day, was in total shock when she walked in—we were off-limits to her for a while after that.

Kevin planned to meet up with Terry and the wheat harvest crew before starting his college work. We would be seeing him and Terry in August when we returned to the States for a McCarthy family reunion in Michigan.

That same numbing feeling came over me as I watched him board the plane—this was by far the most difficult phase of my life.

In August of 1971, our family went to the States for home leave. I went a few days early with the younger children—we needed to buy clothes for everyone: we took the empty duffel bags along to be refilled. I wanted to get that done before we went to Michigan for the reunion with Terry's family. We took Flint, our macaw, with us too.

We hadn't visited the French island of Guadeloupe or flown with Air France in their Caravelle plane—it was a smaller plane and flew at a lower altitude with a much better view of the ocean around the islands.

We landed at Guadeloupe early afternoon, boarded a shuttle for the hotel. I gave the driver the name of our hotel as we boarded—it was the first one we saw after we started off. He didn't show any sign of stopping.

"Sir, that's our hotel."

Instead of stopping, the driver continued on—I reminded him again. He ignored me and stopped at all the hotels along the long road around the entire island. Brigid, who tends to get airsick and carsick, was looking a little green as we stopped and started so many times. We finally arrived back where we started at our hotel—the driver stopped this time and stood outside the door waiting for us to disembark; Brigid was the first one off. She threw up right in front of him—need I say more.

The rooms at the hotel left much to be desired—the bed had the old-fashioned spring and mattress. We settled in; Flint was let out of his cage and walked under the bed to go to sleep (he always slept under Sean's bed at home). At 5:00 p.m. we headed down to the restaurant for dinner—the sign blocking the doorway stated dinner is served at 8:00. All of us were tired and hungry—we looked around outside for shops that might sell food of some sort; we came up with crackers and that was it.

At 8:00 we were standing at the entrance of the restaurant and were assigned a large round table in the center. People came in and filled the smaller tables all around us—waiters filled their orders while we sat and waited. Finally, after much urging on my part, the waiter brought soup to start the meal; nothing after that—other patrons were eating their dessert and there we sat. The little ones laid their heads on the table and fell asleep. I woke them and as we were leaving, the man at the register came running after us.

"You cannot leave until you sign this slip—the cost of the meal goes with the hotel room and you must sign it."

"Sir, we sat there for an hour with a bowl of soup—I will not sign anything that states we have received a meal."

We continued up the stairs with the man shouting after us. In the room, I sat on the bed—Flint let out a raucous call as the spring sank down on him. Luckily, he escaped without any harm—so much for the shape of that bed.

The next morning, back at the airport, the clerk at the ticket counter said I couldn't leave until I signed the meal ticket.

"We didn't receive a meal and I refuse to sign it."

A gentleman standing behind me in line walked to the counter and said:

"I was there at the restaurant last night and saw how badly this lady and her children were treated—they did not receive a meal and she does not have to sign for it."

The clerk checked the children and me on the flight—I thanked the gentleman who came to our aid; so much for wanting to see the French island.

The rest of the flight to the States was beautiful. The shades of blue of the ocean around the islands were breathtaking.

From Florida, we took Delta Airline to Houston, Texas. When we deplaned there, we waited in the baggage area for them to bring Flint to us. Suddenly, we heard Flint's desperate calls and he and his cage came flying through the baggage chute—part of his long tail hung desolately out the cage. Poor Flint was so indignant and let everyone know it—he was so glad to see us. The airline apologized for not hand-carrying his cage as they had promised.

Trans Texas airline then took us to Bryan, TX—the plane is very small so Flint was in sight of us in the little baggage compartment behind out seats. When we landed in Bryan, a lady at the airport there was staring at Flint.

"Did you paint him or was he born that way?"

"He was born that way, ma'am."

The next day we were at the Sears store when it opened—all the summer clothes were on sale and that was the only kind we needed. We spent the entire time with the same clerk as we went from one department to another. The younger children were amazed that the store didn't close down at noon for a couple of hours as they did in Suriname. As we left, the clerk shook our hands.

"You have made my day."

Terry flew to Houston with Rory, Bob and Cronan (Terry Jr. and Kevin were on harvest crew in the States). There he rented a nice new American Motors station wagon—he had requested a van from the rental agency: this was the largest they had. They met up with us in Bryan.

Our plans were for an easy drive to northern Michigan and along the way visit relatives and friends. Terry was also looking for an airplane to buy—in the four-month period in the Aero Club, he accumulated only 16.25 hours of flying: this could be a dead-end street.

Our first stop was Oklahoma City to get information regarding the registration in the United States of the PA 18 Piper Cub we bought in Suriname—then on to Missouri to see my relatives where Terry looked at a plane for sale.

In Michigan, one of the stops was Charlevoix, a town not too far from Petoskey. Terry looked at a Cessna 182 there; he took the address and phone number of the owner. He met with the owner—the log books were the originals and everything was in order. He bought the plane with the sale to be finalized before we left—it would be delivered to Florida where the owner had his winter home; Terry would pick it up at a later date.

Our final destination was a cabin on Crooked Lake near Petoskey, MI—Grandpa McCarthy had rented the cabin for us. When he rented it, the snow was so deep only the roof could be seen—now it was a beautiful sight near the sparkling water of the lake. What a perfect place for the family reunion.

A few days later, Terry Jr. and Kevin arrived at the Pellston Airport near Crooked Lake and joined us—it was so good to see them again. What a great week-long Irish reunion we had. Grandpa Robert and Grandma, Minnie McCarthy, Terry's sister Ginny and husband Gene Hutchings and family living in nearby Petoskey, another sister, Dolores and husband, Gerri Woltanski and children from Kent City, MI, brother Robert and daughters from Virginia and brother, Gene and wife Barb and children from Massachusetts.

The lake water was still a little cool for us but did not deter the children very long. The fireplace in the cabin did feel good though in the evenings as we sat around and told "war stories" and brought the family up-to-date on everything.

The boys took GED tests in Petoskey—they passed the test so the correspondence courses did their job. The children and I had our annual physicals at a local clinic in Petoskey.

Terry's physical was a little more complicated—his appointment for it at Little Traverse Hospital coincided with finalizing the purchase of the plane. George Hartman, the owner, brought the purchase agreement to the hospital. There, George found Terry in his backwards smock, gave him the agreement to read and sign: between coughing, giving specimens, having specimens taken, weighing in, being measured, etc., he managed to read it. George found two nurses who were willing to put their names down as witnesses so the agreement was signed and the plane was finally purchased.

A few days later, we went to the Pellston airport, turned in the rented station wagon and were ready to return to Suriname. Grandpa McCarthy was the only one who braved the early morning, thirty-five-mile drive to the airport—we were so happy to see him as he was equally happy and sad to see us off.

We stopped to change planes in Chicago, then to Miami and down the Caribbean to Paramaribo. It was a great vacation—we covered a lot of miles, saw a lot of people, did a lot of things and now owned an airplane.

The Paranam Works

A stalagmite of aluminum
Stands on my table near the wall,
a cone resembling a small pine tree—
boughs totally enveloped
in a shimmering blanket of ice.
What cave or cavern would yield
the likes of this—
a stalagmite of aluminum?

I wondered this when a man,
whose features
denoted an ancestral background
much different than mine,
presented it to me:
"Aluminum drippings fashioned it
in 'Castings' at the Paranam Works."

In the years since then
I have listened to this man and others
listened and watched and found
that the Paranam Works of Suralco in
the country of Suriname is
too simple a statement, belying
the ultimate impact of sights seen
that whisper of the goals men
set, challenged, then conquered.

How can one, fresh in this country,
be prepared to see the Paranam Works
after driving past rice paddies,
jungle huts, swamps, more jungle?
Yet there it stands, work of the 20th century
master, where once jungle reigned.

Master, but a wise and gentle one
dwelling side by side
with Bush Negro hut, Javanese rice paddy
Chinese merchant, Hindustani farm—
not harming the customs of their cultures—
enhancing them with its bold contrast.

Master, because in times long past
men of one country spoke to men of another
each with their different source of wealth
together, they spoke, planned, worked—
became discouraged, lost hope
then picked up and started over again.

Master, because men of many colors and creeds
stood in water and jungle to explore, survey
what the earth had hidden below.
Master, because more of these men
took machines and amidst water and cayman
built roads to open the face of the earth.

What manner of men these, who operate
the monstrous 1350 crane
with rhythm and poise, to
strip off the soil to lay bare the bauxite?
What manner of men these, who take other machines—
dig deep into the earth to fill lesser monsters:
Euclid trucks, to feed the machines
other men use to refine the raw bauxite?

What manner of men took more machines
through more jungle and built roads
to harness a river and channel its power
so that other men could take
"refined" bauxite and through smelting
and casting, bring forth shiny ingots and bars?

What manner of men?—men of all nationalities,
walks of life, who blend their talents
so that the pulsing jungle drums
set the tempo for the throbbing machines
and from the gaping face of the mine
products are born to be shared by all men.

Shared by the men who
sail the ships up the Suriname River
from all parts of the world
to the dock at the Paranam Works
seeking out what best suits their needs
bauxite, alumina, aluminum
and receiving their fill
depart, bringing a part of us all over the globe.

So if you see my gift standing here
look at the shadow it casts
to the men who worked in the past,
the brightness of it beckoning
to train, perfect and expand their work
so a new generation will hold out a hand
to a friend from another land
with a new gift fashioned
from "aluminum drippings" at
The Paranam Works.

Chapter VIII

The 182 Comes to Suriname

Terry's original plan to just go for the private license changed when his instructor said going directly for the commercial license was possible. At that time, the instrument rating was not a part of the commercial license. He went to the States on some business and stopped in at Opa Locka airport in Florida on the way. He checked into a ground school class there for a quick brush-up and then took the written commercial test—he had decided to bypass the written private test. When he received the results later in Paranam, he missed passing by one point.

Now in preparing to bring the 182 down to Suriname from Punta Gorda, Florida, he needed to include a lot of work preparing to retake the commercial license test along with the preparations for the actual flight. Many charts were needed to make out the flight plan for that flight.

When all the charts were accumulated in Paranam, it became almost a nightly ritual to cover the living room floor with them to work on the flight plan for the trip. All the family was involved in this operation—we learned a lot of geography in a short time.

After a couple of months of this, Terry and his flight instructor, Bob Smith, felt they were ready for the trip. They took a commercial flight to Miami, rented a car and went to Punta Gorda to pick up the plane. From there, Opa Locka airport was their first stop.

Terry again took the commercial license test. He passed the test. Leaving Opa Locka airport, they flew out over open water, nothing but water visible in every direction as far as they could see. (Terry still feels his stomach flip when remembering that sight as it did the day he actually saw it.) They were on their way to Suriname via the Caribbean Islands.

The schedule called for their first overnight in Santo Domingo, Dominican Republic. We received a telegram from Terry the second night—they were on the Island of St. Vincent. Everything was fine; they were scheduled to arrive at Zanderij Airport the next day after a stop for fuel at Port of Spain, Trinidad, and Georgetown, Guyana.

We received a very welcome call late the next day asking for a ride home—it was dark when the call came. I knew the Zanderij Airport was on IFR after sunset—they landed just before sunset. They were home!

The 182

The plane was left at Zanderji Airport for a day and then flown to Zorg en Hoop airport in Paramaribo. There it occupied a space with the Cessna Skymaster Father Calis flew into the interior missions. He was happy to share the hangar with Terry. The rent money was paid in U.S. dollars to a U.S. bank—that gave PAS a dollar account to buy parts and supplies in the US.

Terry set up a work bench and tools along with other supplies in the hangar—he could walk away each time without having to clean up everything before leaving. The PAS mechanic servicing the Skymaster worked well with Terry also.

Now the work began—the 182 was disassembled and stripped of its coats of paint. All the spare time afforded Terry and the boys was spent with the plane.

When it came time to paint it, Terry found a shop in downtown Paramaribo that was able to do the actual painting. The owner of the shop offered to do the work on Sunday. This allowed Terry to transport parts of the plane to the shop early Sunday mornings before the traffic got heavy. He used our VW van for transporting the various parts. The fuselage was first on the list—the back part was placed inside the van with the tripod landing gear resting on the street. Rory sat in back of the van and kept watch over it. The wings and the tail section were transported in similar fashion.

White was the only color used. The shop owner did an excellent job. When all the parts were back at the hangar, the plane was reassembled and ready for use. Rory, Bob and Cronan worked with Terry through it all—that's probably why some of them followed aviation in their adult lives.

One thing I associate with the work on the plane was the introduction of a fast-food place to the family. One of the boys went to a food stand near the hanger to get something for lunch one day. He ordered *roti met kip* for all of us (roasted chicken wrapped in roti, similar to a tortilla) and brought it back to the hangar. The first bite brought tears to our eyes and a run for a drink of water. Javanese spices were a little too much. The owner of the stand made special ones for us after that.

Quite often Father Calis came in—his plane was rolled out and off he'd go to one of the outlying mission landing strips. There's nothing quite like the roar of a push-pull engine as it's taking off.

Another Thanksgiving rolled round. Thanksgiving dinners were held for the Americans at the staff club in Paranam. Suralco requested the help of one of the wives to oversee the preparations for the celebration each year—no limit to the amount of money spent.

This year the task fell to me. The dining room of the staff club was not large enough for all the families to eat at one time—previous years, the dinner was served in shifts: not too pleasant for the families or the chef.

A large screened-in dance hall was connected to the staff club at a lower level. Why not use that to accommodate everyone at one sitting? I enlisted the help of some of the wives. Cindy Duerlo, a teacher at the American school, made red-checkered curtains for each of the partitions of the screened-in area along with matching table cloths. We had twelve long tables—Lou Morris, Javanese wife of an American employee, collected kerosene lamps from her Javanese friends and relatives to light each table.

Our menu included shrimp cocktail, turkey, stuffing, mashed potatoes, cranberry sauce, corn, fresh baked loaves of bread, pumpkin pie with whipped cream. The cooks in the kitchen said they could take care of the turkeys, potatoes, corn, cranberry sauce and the pie crusts but not the pumpkin pie filling and the shrimp.

I bought pumpkin (*papoen*) at the open-air market and cooked it. Lou, a fantastic cook, ordered and ultimately prepared the shrimp along with her wonderful sauce. The local bakery baked the loaves of bread for each table— these could be served on bread boards and cut there.

Thanksgiving morning, I came to the kitchen with my prepared pumpkin filling (looking very soupy as it always does with the eggs, milk and spices added) and started filling the prepared pie crusts awaiting me.

One cook, who made the crusts, looked at the filled crusts and said: "That's alright, Missy, I put something in to make it thick."

"Oh no, you don't, they'll be fine," I answered as I opened the preheated oven and started placing the pies on the shelves.

He looked very sad—his eyes turned to amazement though as I took the pies out later, all firmly set. During the course of the day, I periodically checked into the kitchen to see how things were progressing and make some suggestions along the way—by afternoon, the cooks hid when they saw me coming. Later in the afternoon, it was evident that I needed to recruit Rory and Bob to help peel potatoes.

That evening, the dance hall was transformed into a beautiful dining room, the kerosene lamps softly lighting the tables. The pool table at one end of the hall, covered with a cloth, held all the fresh fruits, nuts and goodies. A shrimp cocktail stood at each place setting.

A consultant for a heavy equipment company in the States happened to come into the staff club about that time. He stood by the railing on the upper level.

"Wow, that is a gorgeous sight—wait till I get my camera, I gotta get a picture of this."

We set another place for him.

After grace was said, the waiters brought in a roasted turkey to be carved at each table, a loaf of bread on the bread board for slicing, bowls of mashed potatoes, stuffing, gravy and corn—later came the pie with whipped cream and coffee. It was quite a family gathering.

A day in December, Terry brought home the mail as usual when he came home for lunch—wow, a letter from Kevin. Inside was a brochure about enlisting in the Marines. I started reading it as Terry ate his lunch—*surely, Kevin, you're not thinking of that.* I continued reading the brochure as I walked out to the top of the back stairs to wave good-bye to Terry—there on the back page of the brochure: "Forget it, Mom, I already did."

"Oh no," I yelled as I threw the brochure down to Terry.

"Hang on there, Mother, it'll be all right."

I began reading the letter. He received his Lottery Draft number, 46—he opted to dodge the draft and enlist in the Marines December 20, 1971. After our reunion in August in Michigan, Kevin returned to Bryan, Texas, where he worked at the Read Meat Packing Company as he had done while in high school—he took night classes at Blinn Community College.

Now we were sending letters to Kevin in boot camp in San Diego—he went so far away so soon. Years later, he told me how homesick he was then as he saw the Christmas decorations on the homes in the hills around San Diego and saw the pictures I sent him of our Crib scene in Paranam.

He wanted to be in the engineers in the Marine Corps—apparently, his six-foot-seven-inch frame said military police to them. He served in Okinawa and Korea as well as in the States and four years later, with the rank of sergeant, returned to civilian life.

Kevin called his grandfather, Bob McCarthy (also a marine in WWI), one day after he made sergeant: "Hello, Cpl. McCarthy, this is Sgt. McCarthy"—he couldn't resist that.

Early the next year, on a Friday, in the late afternoon, we loaded up the van with fishing gear and food and took off for Afobaka Dam about seventy kilometers south of Paranam—the fishing is good in the lake behind the dam. There's also good game fishing in the tailraces by the dam.

Many of the world's aluminum smelters operate on electrical energy from hydropower and this is the case in Suriname. The Brokopondo Project made it possible for Suralco to have a fully integrated aluminum industry at Paranam—Suriname made the natural resource (the Suriname River) available and Suralco provided the capital and technical knowledge to develop the resource. The lake was a byproduct of this and furnished a beautiful recreation area.

Upon our arrival at the lake, we settled into the cabin and checked in with the guide providing the boat. The older boys went out on the lake the next morning—they returned at noon with a nice catch of tukanari, a fish resembling trout.

"It's really great out there," said Rory, "you'll love it."

"There's a lot of piranha too," added Cronan, "they're kinda scary."

"Come and have lunch now. You can clean the fish afterwards—we'll have a good fish fry for dinner."

After lunch, Brigid, Hilary, Camille, Terry and I went out to fish. The guide handled the boat very well and took us far out into the lake. We reached a little cove and got our fishing rods ready. The children were sitting in front of me in the boat and had their lines into the water as I prepared my rod. Camille began tugging her line.

"I think I got one!"

The next thing I knew a piranha, teeth snapping, sailed by my face and landed on the bottom of the boat near me, flapping and snapping. Camille sat there with a startled look—the guide was laughing as he killed the fish.

"Next time, don't swing your catch by my face, okay."

"We won't," came the chorus.

One of the tukanari we caught had a bite out if its tail—I guess he wasn't quite fast enough when a piranha struck.

The guide kept looking at the gathering clouds.

"We go now, *aling kom*." (The rain was coming.)

The fishing tackle was stored and we took off. We literally flew across the water which was churned up by the wind, the bow slapping down between waves. Then the rain came down in sheets. The docks on shore were a welcome sight when they came into view. Needless to say, we were soaked to the skin and shivering as we climbed out the boat.

Now I knew why there was a fireplace in the cabin—I thought the fireplace looked odd here in the tropics when we first arrived. Terry got a fire going and after a nice hot shower, we were ready to fry the fish for dinner. We even froze some and took them home in our cooler.

We spent some time touring the dam itself—Camille turned a little pale as we walked across the open-grid floor of the bridge across the river by the dam. Looking down through the holes was a little too much for her.

It was fun watching some men standing on the side of the tailraces trying to catch the tarpon that came up the river—the tarpon fed on the fish that at times came through the tailraces from the lake: the fish were stunned after bouncing through the tailrace and were an easy catch for the tarpon. Not too many tarpon were actually caught but it was a delight to watch the fish dancing on their tail fighting to free themselves when snagged by a hook. They snatched at anything that looked like food.

The older boys went out again the next morning; after lunch we were on our way back to Paranam with the rest of our fish and lots of memories.

Terry had a clerk in the mine office named Muny who was very efficient—Terry really appreciated his work. Muny was a Bush-Negro. In the middle of the eighteenth century, the white settlers were at the peak of their prosperity and lived in luxury while the slaves worked under extremely bad conditions. To escape the ill-treatment, the Bush-Negro fled into the jungle in sizeable numbers and banded together to protect their freedom. They organized themselves into tribes of free people in their villages and still live that way.

Muny invited Terry and me to a festival in his village. The best way he could describe the festival to us was that it was a ritual honoring his guardian angel. With music and drums, they performed the ritual which was very interesting—a feast of wonderful food followed the performance.

All the villagers then gathered on the pavilion and began dancing to music in a "follow the leader" style—they went round in a circle, not with partners, just each doing their own thing by themselves. They invited us to join them which I did—I had a great time. We felt honored by Muny's invitation.

Another school year was coming to an end. In May of 1972, Rory returned to the States for college. He originally planned to leave later in the year but decided to spend the summer with Terry Jr. on the harvest crew in Texas to earn money before registering for college. The younger children and I were in Costa Rica at the time so we didn't see him off. However, I knew he would come home to Paranam for Christmas.

Father Calis also made trips to some missions that were located on rivers in the area. He requested permission to take Cronan and Hilary (whom he called Sam) on a week's river trip to some of those missions—Hilary was nine, Cronan fifteen at the time. They wanted to go so a date was set.

I drove them to the designated meeting place: a little town on the Essequibo River where the boat was anchored. It was quite a large boat with a cabin and inboard motor—larger than I expected; two men were standing on deck. Father Calis was waiting for us in a little store near the dock. He joined Hilary and Cronan and boarded the boat while Chris, Brigid, Camille and I stood on the dock waving good-bye as they started upriver.

A week later we, plus Hilary's friend Bruce Deci, stood on the dock as the boat approached. Hilary and Cronan were waving excitedly when they saw us. Besides their belongings, each carried a beautiful clay water jug as they walked toward us—the jars were gifts from the Indians.

Father Calis said they were good travelers who would have lots of tales to tell. Bruce was so happy to see Hilary and immediately offered to share his cold can of Coke with him—Hilary to this day remembers that. A Coke was quite a luxury at that time.

The two of them shared their stories with us all the way home. The first Indian village was quite a short distance upriver; two nuns and a brother lived there with the villagers. A large flock of multi-colored macaws flew over as they arrived—their raucus calls and brilliant colors made quite an impression on them. It was dark, in the jungle that's really dark, before they reached their next destination: a spotlight was used to make the mooring. They spent the night in the village; the other men stayed on the boat. One of them came running up later asking for help. They were fishing off the boat and hooked a fish so big they needed help to bring it in.

"Mom, it was a big catfish, about thirty-five pounds," Cronan said.

"The men gutted it and cut it into steaks," added Hilary, "they didn't even skin it. We took some with us to share with people in the other villages the next day."

"In the morning, we began walking to other villages. We started in the jungle, broke out into a savanna, then back into more jungle." Hilary became very excited just thinking about it.

"Mom, when we got to a certain point in the jungle, one of the Indians with us hit a tree trunk several times with his walking stick—it made a funny sound."

"Yeah, then we came into the village—not one person was seen anywhere," interrupted Cronan.

"We just stood there quietly and soon we saw heads poking out from behind trees all around us—then the children came running followed by the adults. They were really glad to see us."

"We visited several villages. The boat was waiting for us at one of the villages on a smaller river. We slept in hammocks on the boat and it was fun swaying back and forth in them."

"I was sleepwalking one night," Hilary admitted. "It's a good thing Father Calis caught me."

"When we came to another village on the river, there was a dugout canoe pulled onto shore," added Cronan, "a lot of people were standing around looking into it."

They were looking at a deer one of the men killed—it was so tiny it looked like a dog. We learned that's as big as they get there in Suriname.

Now as we approached our house, they admitted it was an exciting trip but they were glad to be home again.

We kept in touch with Father Calis after our return to the States. When his letters stopped coming, we learned he was killed returning home in his Jeep from one of the villages: he collided head-on with a truck at a corner in the road.

As Christmas approached, we prepared the Crib in the living room—the shepherds and sheep were in their places in the little field, Mary and Joseph were in the cave with the cow and donkey as they awaited the birth of Jesus. The artificial tree would be arriving with Rory—his flight had been delayed. I decided not to fight it this year—trying to get a real tree here was next to impossible.

Rory and the tree arrived late Christmas Eve—we were constructing and decorating the tree into the wee hours of Christmas morning. It was a beautiful tree; we still have it.

Rory wrote about his adventure with that tree—it explains why we were decorating the tree into the wee hours of Christmas morning.

Rory

Christmas "Oughta-See"

It seemed like a simple request from Mom. After all, how difficult is it to bring a boxed artificial Christmas tree with me when I come home for Christmas vacation, even if Mom and Dad and the family live in Suriname?

What did surprise me, though, was that Mom finally decided to get an artificial tree. Christmas "musts" were the crib with all the trimmings and a real pine tree.

I left my home in Suriname in May, 1972. I planned to fly to Bryan, Texas, to get a driver's license and then head north to meet Terry, who was working with a wheat harvest crew for the summer—he was to be my guide for the first season.

Having driven only on the left side of the road in Suriname and never with a column shift as the truck I borrowed had, I flunked the first test miserably. After finally passing the driving test, I tried for a commercial license. This time, I borrowed a van with an automatic transmission and passed by the thinnest of margins.

Tracking down the harvest crew, which traveled from Texas to the Dakotas, was no small task. I found them and gave Terry his mail from Bryan: one letter from Texas A&M stated that if he did not return for summer school, he could not return at all. After making a few rounds around the wheat field in the combine with me, Terry left to go to summer school—so much for being my guide for the summer.

In September, I rode the bus from Texas to the University of Missouri-Rolla. At the admission office, I felt the extreme loneliness of making a decision to spend four or five years of my life here in Rolla.

After completing my first semester, I was again in Bryan on my nineteenth birthday, December 18, 1972, ready to shop for the Christmas tree. It proved a great time to shop for trees because they were all on sale. One problem though—less money bought a bigger tree, so why not get the biggest tree (six feet); not a wise decision when you're traveling by air to South America. At the same time, I worked on getting my airline tickets.

"You want to go WHERE for Christmas vacation on such short notice?" They did find a way to grant my request though.

With the tree and the ticket in tow, Terry drove me to Houston to catch my flight to Suriname. In the terminal, the six-foot tree in the box stood out like a grain elevator on the wheat-covered Kansas prairie—instead of being a guidepost to the young, eager-to-please, but disoriented harvester that the elevator was, the box scattered people like flies off a dead armadillo on a Texas highway when a car goes by.

It was the height of the hijacking era; I was very nervous about going on board with the presents I carried. I tried not to have shifty eyes that might draw the attention of well-trained police to search me and confiscate the Lionel freight train we older boys bought for the young kids at home for Christmas.

I might have been better off if the police had taken the freight train though—I think the train tipped off the sky caps when we landed in San Juan, Puerto Rico. They were quick to make the connection between the grain elevator-sized box, with which I was forlornly stranded, and what it would take to move it. What the heck, I had eighteen hours to coax one of them to move it through the construction-riddled terminal. I tried to move it myself but the airline people wouldn't keep my carry-on luggage behind the counter long enough for me to do so.

Just as the strange currents and eddies of a river finally conspire to catch a log behind a large boulder where thousands of logs had passed before, an unsuspecting sky cap got caught behind my Christmas tree box in the middle of a river of people. For the few brief seconds that he was thus entangled, I convinced him of the box's content and that his loading of it onto his cart would not deprive him of the ability to father future generations of children. This accomplished, we agreed (I use "we" very loosely) that $10 was just compensation. As the donkey load, ages ago, was lightened by the thought of the very special cargo of Mother and Child, so the spirit of Christmas lightened the load of the sky cap and moved him to charge only $5.

Since money was as thin as my patience, I sat out the remainder of the eighteen-hour layover in Puerto Rico instead of getting a room.

The other three passengers and I—hopefully the tree also—finally boarded the plane for Suriname. We received individual service on board—plenty of food offered to me each time the attendant came by. Although we usually have ham for Christmas dinner, I felt like a stuffed turkey long before the flight ended. I finally went to sleep and dreamed of putting the huge box in our VW bus and enjoy the ride home from the airport.

That was only a dream; my first hint of this reality was Dad's paling face as the luggage system gave birth to the monster tree. The Herculean effort made by my friends Mike Reeder and Herman Landsman to come to the airport on a *bromfiets* (motorbike) at midnight on Christmas Eve had to be duplicated and surpassed when it came time to load the tree into our VW bug instead. Mike and Herman politely left for home when loading began. They may have gone back to call in reinforcements if we didn't shown up in twenty-four hours.

I don't know if bad memories numbed my mind or if the loading was so easy that it wasn't worth remembering—the next thing I knew we were putting the color-coded branches into the color-coded holes in the front room at home. Although not yet decorated, the first, and as yet only, artificial tree made its debut in our family, arriving with Santa Claus on Christmas Eve, 1972.

Terry's work with Alcoa was coming to an end—we knew we'd be starting for home in the near future. About the same time, Suralco decided to put in more docks on the Suriname River. DeFaria's house had already been razed, in fact, they moved a part of it to a plot of land on which their new house was located.

We packed a good part of our belongings while still living in the house. This was stored until we left. Our family moved into two trailers by the staff club. It was hard to leave the house we had grown to love—we certainly didn't like to think of it being torn down. The beautiful hardwood floors, the long row of "crank-open" windows by the dining room and living room that let in the cool breeze from the river had been a loved part of our life: they will live on in our memories.

Terry arranged a Bush Negro group to perform a Fire Dance during that time. They used the house we vacated a day in advance to prepare for it. I went there several times during the day and saw how they psych themselves up for the dance. I don't know what they use for their potions but I didn't like to see that.

It also took a long time to prepare the coals for the fire. This was done in an open area near the staff club. We invited all the expatriates for dinner at the staff club preceding the dance. The local menu included peanut soup, shish kabobs served with a variety of sauces (*my favorite was peanut sauce)* and nasi goring, a rice and chicken dish.

The dance itself was spectacular. The beating of the drums and the chanting seemed to have a trance-like effect on the dancers as they slowly danced on the glowing coals with bare feet. It was fascinating but not something I would want to see again.

Jane stayed with us until the end of our sojourn—she didn't care for the air-conditioned trailers though; she said it made the air too dry. We exchanged Christmas letters for many years. When they stopped coming, our efforts to find out why were not successful.

Chapter IX

Mission Accomplished

The local men Terry trained now completely took over the training operation—it was time for us to move on: departure date, May 6, 1973. Our duffel bags were filling, our belongings were boxed for shipping—our destination: Union, Missouri, a few miles south of my hometown of Washington, Missouri.

Our stay in Suriname did not afford my quest for a ride in an open-cockpit plane. I will continue to pursue it though.

Two of my sisters, Georgia Schroeder and Beatrice Stowe, lived in Union. Georgia's husband, Tony, was in real estate and could find a house for us to rent. Bea's husband, Carl, the postmaster, graciously accepted the job of providing the vehicles needed to pick us up on our arrival at Lambert Field in St. Louis about fifty miles east of Union. Bob, Cronan, Chris, Brigid, Hilary, Camille and I, plus our macaw, Flint, were flying commercial—Terry was flying the 182 back to the States.

Before we left Suriname, Terry flew the 182 to Georgetown, Guyana, for an interview—the mine in Guyana was interested in him doing some training for them. He returned on May 5 to see us off.

"I'm going back to Guyana for a few weeks—I want to check out in detail what they're offering me."

"So, you don't know when you'll return to the States."

"I'll be home for our wedding anniversary, June 14th. Make a reservation at a hotel in St. Louis for the occasion."

"Okay, I'll do that."

"When I get into the States, I'll call you to let you know what time I expect to circle Georgia's house in Union—then you can pick me up at the St. Clair airport."

Some friends also came to the airport to bid farewell—they were sad to see us leave because in the past, when the McCarthys came to see them off on various trips, it always meant an "instant crowd"—they were going to miss that. Our neighbor, Keetsha, in his usual dramatic fashion, cried:

"Don't leave me, Mommy—I won't have any more banana pies."

The last we heard from him was about a year later—he called us when he visited relatives in the States.

Our return itinerary included stops at some of the islands before landing at Puerto Rico where Bob would leave us and continue on to Houston, Texas, to meet up with the older boys.

At Jamaica, the flight was delayed a long time—an irate passenger there was bumped because the flight was oversold. He caused enough ruckus that our plane couldn't leave. I could see we would not make it in time for Bob's flight from Puerto Rico and wondered what we would do.

When we finally arrived at the airport in Puerto Rico, the terminal was pure pandemonium—long lines formed at the counters as the passengers tried to get their flights rescheduled. We stood there looking around, wondering what to do. We needed to start by finding another flight for Bob to Houston. Out of nowhere, a man from one of the ticket counters approached us.

"Where are you going from here?"

"My son, Bob, needs to go to Houston, the other children and I to Miami."

"There's another flight leaving for Houston in a few minutes over here—when he didn't show for the first flight to Houston, I thought you probably were delayed somewhere. His baggage is here—I'll take him to the gate and get him onboard. You go on and don't worry."

God always took care of us.

As usual, we had to clear customs in Puerto Rico. Here we ran into trouble. Flint needed special clearance.

"The man who checks the birds isn't here today."

"I have all the papers duly validated in Suriname for Flint—there's a lot more papers for him than for all the rest of us."

"I'm sorry but that man isn't here today—we'll keep the bird here until tomorrow. When he's duly checked out, we'll send him to you in the States."

"No way will we leave Flint behind. We'll just spend the night right here with him until the man comes tomorrow to check him out."

"You can't do that, ma'am."

"If you don't have anyone here today to take care of us, we will stay here until someone comes."

So Flint and all of us sat down and waited. Before long, the man approached us.

"We've located the man—he's on his way here."

He arrived and found all the papers in order.

"What is your final destination?"

"Union, Missouri."

"I will notify them of your clearance here—they'll come and check you and the bird when you reach your destination."

With all this delay, we rescheduled a flight to Miami—the arrival time: midnight—a room was reserved for us at the hotel at the airport. I couldn't call Carl in Missouri from Puerto Rico; instead, I sent a telegram informing him of the new arrival date.

A group of very weary travelers arrived in Miami at midnight—as Flint was handed to us at the baggage level, I asked Sean to wait a while in that area with Flint.

"Sean, we'll take the elevator to the lobby and get the key to our rooms— I don't think it's a good idea for the people in the lobby to see Flint with us. You can come right up to our room, hopefully alone in the elevator."

"Okay, Mom."

We took the elevator to the lobby, waited in line to get our key, walked back to the elevator, punched the button, the door opened—yes, there stood Sean with Flint. We smiled at the people waiting with us, walked in, closed the door and went to our rooms—so much for trying to plan things.

In the morning we were off to St. Louis. There, Carl with a van he borrowed from a friend and Bea in their car were waiting for us. I was forever indebted to them—they had not received my telegram and came in to St. Louis both days to pick us up. What a wonderful pair!

We sort of "farmed out" the children to my sisters' and brothers' homes until Tony found a house for us to rent. The children enjoyed meeting aunts and uncles and cousins they didn't remember ever meeting before. Brigid, Hilary,

Camille and I along with Flint stayed with my mom—she had nice trees in the yard for Flint. A few days after we arrived at Mom's, a veterinarian came and checked Flint and his papers and found all in order.

One day during that time, I was stopped at a roadblock where the police were checking everyone's driver's licenses. I only had an international driver's license at the time—he accepted it and said he had never had one presented to him before.

Tony found the perfect house for us just a half block from their home—there was a nice tree in the front yard for Flint too. Many people, walking by the house in the following days, stopped and looked around when Flint greeted them with his "Da."

He knew that Georgia was afraid of him and delighted in hollering at the top of his lungs as she came up the sidewalk from her house—he'd move to lower branches to scare her. Sometimes we put him on the railing on the back steps of the house. He soon learned that when he got bored there he could push the little button near the door with his beak and somebody always came to the door to rescue him.

We didn't have a car yet so when the children and I went grocery shopping, we used the cart from the store to bring the food home—we returned the empty cart to the store. We used the same method of transportation on our trips to the Laundromat.

One day as we made our way home, a police car pulled up alongside us.

"Excuse me, ma'am—why aren't these children in school?"

"Oh, we just moved here from Suriname—the school year was completed there before we left."

"Okay, I just needed to check on that. Thank you."

A few days later, the students from a nearby special needs school took an afternoon walk with their teachers down our street. Flint liked kids and got all excited when he saw them coming, hollered and did a little dance from his perch in the tree.

One of the teachers came to the door.

"Would you bring the bird to school tomorrow morning—the children would like to see it up close."

"Of course I will."

The next day I took him, perched on my hand, into the front office of the school. From there, we could hear some children reading—when Flint heard them he immediately called out his "Da" to them.

"It's the bird, it's the bird," the children shouted.

We had a delightful time in the classrooms. After that, when they came down the street for their walk, they all called out his name and talked to Flint as they came by.

June 13, we joined Bea and Carl and family for a cook-out: they were celebrating their wedding anniversary. Georgia joined us there.

"Have you heard from Terry—didn't you say he'd be here tomorrow for your anniversary?"

"Yeah, he called from Mussel Shoals, Alabama, last night and said he'd be here around noon tomorrow. He'll circle your house before he lands in St. Clair."

At noon the next day, we all gathered in the backyard—Georgia had a bit of a skeptical look on her face. As we chatted, I heard the nice reliable sound of the engine of the 182—there was Terry in the 182 circling the house and wagging his wings. What a sight it was—Dad was home!

St. Clair was a few miles from Union—the airport lay alongside highway I-44, a short distance from the town. Terry was on the ground when we arrived in Georgia's car. He looked so different—he let his beard grow, the first time any of us had seen him with a beard. Soon he was engulfed in hugs and kisses.

At home, we had an anniversary celebration where Cronan presented us with a "Think Big" cookie jar and Sean, a "Good Housekeeping" cookbook— they bought the gifts with some money they earned doing some work for the relatives. I still cherish them. Later in the afternoon, Terry and I left for St. Louis to celebrate our twenty-third wedding anniversary at the Chase Hotel.

We bought a used green pickup truck with a camper shell—the name Zelda was painted on the passenger side and Charlie on the driver's side. We left the names in place: we always called the truck Zelda. Terry went out looking for work—he wasn't satisfied with the offer made by the mine in Guyana.

During the summer months, I was busy canning tomatoes and green beans—my sister's relatives had big gardens and were happy to give the excess produce to me. It brought back memories of all the canning I did in

Michigan when the children were young; I always enjoyed seeing the jars of vegetables and fruits accumulate in the basement there.

September came and the children were enrolled in the local schools. Terry accepted a position at Cat Americas Co., a section of the Caterpillar Headquarters in Peoria, Illinois. He did warranty work with customers of Caterpillar heavy equipment in Central and South America and Canada.

Terry took Zelda to Peoria and left it there—he flew the 182 to Peoria on Sundays, stayed at the YMCA during the week, drove Zelda every day after work looking for a house for us in the Peoria area. He returned home on Fridays in the 182.

He found a partially remodeled 100-year-old farm house on two and a half acres of land in the outskirts of a small town of Elmwood, Illinois about twenty-five miles from Peoria, complete with a red barn and outhouse.

I went with him to check it out.

"This is perfect; plenty of space for a good garden next year and a barn for the calves Sean's always wanted to raise."

"I hope he'll let us butcher them later to put the veal in the freezer."

"He knows that's the only way we could handle them—butcher them while they're still young."

The yard and surrounding lot needed much tender loving care; an old refrigerator, stove and mowers reclined in the yard behind the house amid the tall weeds. With many willing hands, that slowly changed.

Cronan repaired the riding mower left behind. He came by the kitchen window one day on the mower with a big grin on his face as he mowed the lawn. A neighbor, Vernie Steck, joined in and brought a saw to the house for the boys to use to cut down the larger growth near the house—he said he was happy to see the place taking shape. The old fence around the house was removed and now the lawn extended past the garage to the fence of the neighboring barn—a short piece of the old plank fence was left in front of the old red barn which framed it nicely.

St. Patrick's Church was across the road from us which made it possible for us to attend daily Mass—Cronan, Sean and Chris served Mass. Father Sheehan, the Pastor, in the Rosminian Order, was from Ireland—that order of priests came to the States as missionaries to serve the families connected with the railroad.

Terry Jr., Rory and Bob (who did meet up with his brothers in Houston on his flight from Puerto Rico) were on the harvest crew cutting wheat through the Midwest. Terry and I flew the 182 to spend a weekend with them in Ogallala, Nebraska.

We learned what it was like to be a *stubble bum*, the name given them in the towns on their route. They worked into the night until the dew settled in, fell into bed for a few hours and back out again in the morning—they prayed for rain.

One night they came to our room at the motel to take a shower and enjoy the air-conditioned room—I had washed clothes ready for them. I understood why they were known as stubble bums. When I shook their clothes outside their trailer as I gathered them earlier that day, the ground was filled with the wheat stubble. I'm sure the Laundromat owners did not appreciate these clothes in their washers.

We ate dinner one night in the trailer with the crew chief and his wife—she cooked all the meals for the crew. Sometimes the meals were brought out into the field.

One morning I rode with Rory in the combine—he turned the machine over to me on one of the rounds. I'm sure he had quite a time straightening out my zig-zag cut. I came away with a deep respect for the work they do.

Flint ruled sometimes from his perch in the house, in the tree in the yard or the railing on the front porch. He usually accompanied me when I gave slide presentations about Suriname to various clubs in Elmwood that requested it.

Winter set in and we were introduced to the cold winter wind blowing across the open fields to our house—Chris says today that's the only thing he remembers about Illinois: cold freezing wind. Flint was quite indignant about spending the whole day in the house that winter. The day of the first snowfall, the teachers at school let Brigid, Hilary and Camille go to the window during class to see the first snowfall they remembered.

December 22, 1973, Terry was on his way to Billings, Montana, in the 182 to deliver it to the new owner—he sold the plane because he couldn't find hangar space for it; he didn't like seeing it tied down at Mt. Hawley Airport in Peoria in the freezing wind and snow. It was a sad parting from an old dependable friend.

His destination was the Croft Ranch in Billings. Mr. Croft used three townships for his cattle—he owned a Piper Cub for locating the cattle; the 182 would transport the family to the home in each of the townships.

Terry continued to log hours flying by renting a Cessna 172—one trip we took was to my aunt Elizabeth's funeral (my godmother) in Washington, Missouri.

During this latter part of 1973, Terry Jr. was at West Texas University, Kevin was a Marine MP in Okinawa, Rory was at the University of Missouri-Rolla, Bob was at the Spartan School of Aeronautics in Tulsa, Oklahoma, Cronan and Sean in high school here in Elmwood, Chris, Brigid, Hilary and Camille in grade school.

I took a job as editor of the *Elmwood Gazette*, a small weekly newspaper. The paper was published in Roseville, Illinois, about forty miles from Elmwood. I typed the stories on a special typewriter that had symbols on top of each letter. These stories were mailed to Roseville during the week—their printer read the symbols and printed them into columns. I took a lot of black-and-white pictures—Terry developed the film which I sent to the publisher. I usually had the center section of the paper tell a story in pictures.

Wednesdays, I drove to Roseville, cut and pasted the *Gazette*, the *Yates City Banner* and the *Williamsfield Times* (the latter two were small towns near us) and carried the printed papers back with me. They were delivered to the towns the next day—quite demanding work.

That first spring in Elmwood, we looked for someone to plow a big garden for us. We talked to a parishioner one Sunday after Mass—Mr. Barton owned a farm nearby.

"Do you know who we can hire to plow a garden for us?"

"Yeah, I'll be glad to do it for you."

Monday morning he came with a big tractor pulling a big plow—he looked at the part where we wanted the garden, paced it off with a few steps, moved in with his machinery and in a few minutes the rich black soil was exposed.

"How much do we owe you—that's a great job."

"Nothing—I had to come by here with the machinery to work on my other farm anyway."

"Thanks so much."

With some work done by the hand tiller, the garden was planted. It produced prize-winning vegetables for Brigid, Hilary and Camille when they took them to the fall fair—Mom had a cellar full of jars of canned vegetables and strawberry jam, a crock of carrots packed in sand for the winter, another crock full of sauerkraut; the freezer was filling fast with corn on the cob and strawberries. That black Illinois soil was potent.

That first spring also brought sadness into our life. Flint was so tired of being in the house all winter. On a nice rainy spring day, I put him in the tree outside, thinking it was warm enough for him. He had a wonderful time hollering and flapping and shaking his feathers in the rain. However, it wasn't warm enough yet—the veterinarian said he had pneumonia and there was nothing he could do for him. We buried him under the tree. We had saved many of his tail and wing feathers and gave some away. My sister Georgia still has one on display in her living room—one of our nieces told me she attached a pen point on hers and displayed it in an old ink jar.

Rambharos and his wife came from Suriname to visit us. He was one of the men Terry trained down there. He was doing well in the training department at Suralco.

It was their first visit to the States—they were overwhelmed at the size of the country. Some things we took for granted amazed them. One day Terry stopped at the drive-through part of our bank to deposit some cash—they could not imagine how the cubicle with the money disappeared when the button was pushed and then appeared inside the building a second later. That fascinated Rambharos.

They insisted on making *roti met kip* for us because they knew how much we liked it (they held back on the spices for us)—I learned how to make the *roti* too. They were delighted to take a copy of the *Elmwood Gazette* home with them featuring a picture of them along with the story.

Two more of the men Terry trained in Suriname also came to visit us in Elmwood: Larry MacArthur and Alphons Rozenstruik (Rosie)—they too were doing well at Suralco.

Larry was in business for himself when he visited us later in Tucson; Rosie, also in business for himself, still comes to our five-year family reunions here in the States—we adopted him into our family so he's included in the family pictures taken at each reunion.

June 14, 1975, the McCarthy Clan converged in Elmwood to celebrate our twenty-fifth wedding anniversary—what a celebration! It started with a Mass in the morning. In the afternoon we enjoyed our first family hog roast—we still celebrate our anniversary every fifth year with a hog roast.

Terry butchered that first hog in our barn with the help of our children—one of the men from the Caterpillar office, Jose Alvarez, a Cuban, and his wife came to watch. (We later stayed with them in Costa Rica.) Another Cuban from the office, Tony Durance, gave Terry the recipe for a sauce the Cubans inject into all parts of the hog with a horse hypodermic needle before roasting it—the roasted meat is delicious.

During the Bicentennial year of 1976, I was able to run a series on the history of Elmwood in the *Gazette*. The series was titled *My Own—My Native Land*.

Bruce Howard of the Elmwood Museum came into the office one day.

"Would you be interested in doing a series on Elmwood history in the paper?"

"Yes, I certainly would."

"I have many pictures and stories of the pioneer families who settled here. Elmwood participated in the Underground Railroad around the Civil War too. I've always wanted to have a series done in the paper to put on file at the museum."

"I'd be happy to do that—I've always liked history. You supply me with the stories and pictures and we'll print the series."

It turned out well—more pictures and stories were added by readers as we went along.

That same year, Terry decided to leave Cat Americas Company and take short-term contracts in training and maintenance of heavy equipment overseas. It was a difficult decision to make. Terry liked the work at the Caterpillar headquarters in Peoria—he was in contact with dealers in Central and South America and Canada. However, he did better working with them on location than writing them about solutions to their problems. Of course, these new contracts meant longer periods of time away from the family than we were accustomed to but we felt that it was workable.

June 1976 he was in Guatemala on a contract with International Nickel, a Canadian company—they opened a mine in El Estor, a little town on Lake Isabella. This was the first of several years of three-month contracts with International Nickel which stipulated he'd spend one month at home in between the contracts.

Kevin returned to civilian life in 1976 after four years in the Marines. He sent us his tassel after he completed his two-year degree for diesel mechanic in California. He met the love of his life, Micki, in California and brought her home with him—they were married in September. Later that year, the *Elmwood Gazette* was sold to the *Elmwood Shopper*—I was no longer the editor. I began work as a Kelly girl from their office in Peoria.

Now another phase of our life began. Back in 1964, our decision to work hand in hand with families in foreign lands led us to work in Costa Rica for two years—we were convinced a family had so many advantages over single people; men more easily identified with instructors who had families. We continued that work in Suriname. Now we could no longer travel to other lands as a family—we had one son married now—they were starting their own families. We're glad we pursued our goal—it opened new worlds for us. We made many new friends and had many new experiences. Our family has always maintained very close ties even to this day.

Though Terry was away from home more now, the families he met overseas became our good friends—some of their members visited us and ours with theirs. It certainly wasn't always easy—in fact, there were some very difficult times. However, it provided me with the possibility to join him for honeymoons in exotic places.

Chapter X

Life Goes On

Excitement grew as we prepared for the feast of Christmas in 1976—Terry was coming home for a month and some of the boys would make it home on break from college. The crib was in place and looked beautiful basking in the late afternoon sunlight coming through the window in the living room. More and more packages surrounded the tree. The wonderful aroma of cookies baking filled the house. The same peace and serenity reigned as always as we awaited the birth of Jesus—all was quiet and still as we walked through the snow to the church across the road for Midnight Mass on Christmas Eve. In the morning, presents were opened before Mom's cinnamon rolls were served with breakfast—another wonderful Christmas feast.

A few days later, Terry said to me:

"How would you like to fly to Toronto with me?"

"Sounds like a winner to me. I've never been there before."

"It'll probably be much colder there with the wind coming off the lake."

"It can't be much colder than the wind coming across the open land here in Illinois."

Terry had meetings scheduled at the International Nickel office in Toronto, the home office of the nickel mine in Guatemala. Although it was bitterly cold in Toronto, I thoroughly enjoyed the trip. Much of my time was spent in the hotel lobby and the adjacent mall while Terry went to the meetings.

The lobby of the hotel was beautiful—the high ceiling was supported by wooden columns displaying the intricate grain of the wood—the wood-paneled walls used with them gave the whole place a warm glow: Christmas decorations enhanced their beauty. I watched the ladies in their gorgeous fur coats and matching hats coming and going.

In the mall attached to the hotel were restaurants and shops of all sorts making it possible to stay under cover and out of the cold wind from Lake Ontario. Terry had to bundle up in everything he owned when he went out to the meetings.

It was a unique and memorable Christmas gift: the first of our exotic honeymoons with many more to come.

In March of 1977, Terry bought a Cessna 172 while he was home. He planned to fly it to Guatemala with our son Bob as his copilot. The flight plan included stops in Rolla, Missouri, where Rory was attending the university, then on to Oklahoma, Texas, Tapachula, Mexico and their final destination, Aurora Airport in Guatemala City.

They left on a cold cloudy day from Tri-County Airport a few miles from our home. It was a little disconcerting to watch Bob take a long pole and tap the rotating beacon on the tail to get them to work but then they were off to Guatemala.

I received daily calls on their progress, finally a welcome call from Guatemala—they were on the ground there. Bob spent a few days in Guatemala and returned stateside on a commercial flight.

Terry worked nine months in Guatemala with two weeks at home in September and four weeks over Christmas and New Year. The end of this contract was coming up in April—it called for a round trip home before the last two months of the contract.

Why not have Mom go to Guatemala instead of Dad coming home? Camille was twelve years old—we all felt it was time for the young end of the family to assume some independent responsibility. Sean, Chris, Brigid, Hilary and Camille were in school and Bob was living at home. They all admitted that Brigid was a talented cook. It was as good a time as ever for me to go.

I planned to spend the last week in April at the plant site in El Estor, Guatemala—this would give Terry the time to install the rebuilt gyro compass I planned to bring down for the Cessna 172. We could check it out on a flight to the Mayan temple ruins at Tikal before flying down to Carmen's *pension* at Samara Beach in Costa Rica the first two weeks in May.

Since Continental Airline claimed they gave faster, better service when allowed to compete with Ozark Airline in Peoria, I decided to give them a try. At 6:45 a.m. Saturday, April 23, I boarded the flight scheduled to leave for Chicago at 7:00 a.m. At 8:15 a.m., I was still on the ground in Peoria as the crew finally found an adequate source of power to refuel the plane—I barely made the connection on the Eastern flight at 9:00 a.m. to Miami.

A welcoming committee, Dad and two secretaries, Sylvia and Velia, were on hand to greet me in Guatemala City around 5:00 p.m. My suitcase didn't make the connection in Chicago.

As we were leaving the airport in Terry's Toyota pickup, another secretary, Nanette, was spotted hurrying along the walkway to the airport—she and her mother made the trip from home by bus but didn't arrive in time to meet me—another warm greeting followed right there in the street.

In the hotel room, a bouquet of white roses stood on the table. Terry searched the florist shops to no avail and then found the roses in the open-air marketplace: they were very special.

That evening, we had dinner at the home of a family Terry met—a wonderful meal of soup, ham cooked to perfection in a special sauce, black beans, rice and salad. In just a few short hours in the country, I met many of Terry's friends and felt I had known them for a long time.

In the morning, we were off to the airport, this time to take a flight in the 172 to the plant site near El Estor. Signs of the 1976 earthquake were still visible as we flew over the countryside. We landed at Las Dantes Airport—back to the dirt runways we knew in Costa Rica. The plant was alongside the airport but the mine was a couple of kilometers up the mountain. Terry lived in one of the trailers in the company town built alongside the little town of El Estor on the shore of Lake Isabell—this was our home now. The first thing Terry did when we got to the trailer was get a glass of cold milk to drink with the piece of rhubarb pie I brought from home—customs permitted me to keep it for him.

Guatemala was very different from the places we lived before. Many Indians from the surrounding villages worked in the mine. They were very small in stature—the adults came up to my shoulder when they stood alongside me at Mass in the church in El Estor Sunday evening (I'm five feet nine inches). Father Tom Moran, a Claretian priest, from Chicago was the pastor of the church; his Assistant was Father Chris, a priest from England.

Sister Mary, Sister Miriam and Marie Eagan from the States had a clinic near the church. When I visited them, they said they had trouble convincing the people in the States not to compare the height and weight of the Indians with the norms there in the States—the Indians really were in good health though small in stature.

There was some tension between the military and the church here because of the influence the priests had on the Indians. The priest from England went on his rounds on horseback to the villages in the area. (We learned later that he received threats from the military—the bishop advised him to return to England. Not too long after that, a Franciscan priest was assassinated on the other side of the lake.)

The following week was full of activities with a couple of special events. One was a dinner cooked by seven of the secretaries working at the plant site. It was quite delightful listening to seven cooks in the kitchen speaking Spanish a mile a minute while getting all the finishing touches done on the dinner. The meal was delicious—I felt so honored by their wish to do this for me.

The other highlight was a dance featuring a marimba band with a complete brass section and percussion—wow, they hit every little note that could possibly be put in (very much like Kenton does). Their "5th of Beethoven" was the best I've heard.

Early Saturday morning, the 172 took us north from El Estor over a green carpet of jungle broken in a few spots by burned-off vegetation and tiny huts—people homesteading. Then, only dark polka dots were visible on the carpet where clouds left their shadows—a world all to ourselves now—no sign of life—only green jungle in every direction.

Quite suddenly, straight ahead, an ancient city stretched out before us as if awakening from a long sleep, its huge temples majestically guarding the extremities: Tikal, the Mayan city-state—breathtaking!

We landed on the dirt strip—a guide met us and we started on our journey into the past. Temple IV rose 229 feet above us, jungle growing from its sides and its base. Terry used the roots and ladders, held together by baling wire, chains and rocks to climb to the base of the temple. All this growth was left in place when this temple was exposed to enable the visitor to see the extent of the jungle growth that covered the rest of the village and plaza before that excavation was completed.

That mode of entrance to the temple was too formidable for me so I stayed below. I watched a column of ants carrying leaves, much larger than they, in procession toward the base of the temple. Do they alone now bring their offerings to the temple? Bright red and blue auroras, birds native to the area, flashed about in the trees while two monkeys played among the branches.

Twelve hundred years had passed since the Mayans came and worshipped here. We stood in awe of their ability to construct these temples. The limestone was cut with flint stone and pried apart with sticks.

Jungle covers most of the space between Temple IV and the Great Plaza of the North Acropolis. Temples I, II, and III were visible now, reflecting the afternoon sun, as we drove in a van up the Maudsley Causeway. Water once flowed over it into the reservoir assuring the Mayans ample water during the dry season. Nearby was the limestone quarry where they obtained the building material for the temples.

The city-state of Tikal covered 224 square miles with 3,000 buildings—1,000 buildings were in the plaza area of Tikal itself. Their civilization grew and prospered and then declined and was taken over by jungle 500 years before Columbus came to the new world.

There were two tombs in Temple I, the Tomb of the Jade Jaguar. Temple II had no tomb—ninety-six steps gave the visitor a view from the top of this temple. Temple III held the tomb of a priest.

Wild turkeys with the coloring of peacocks and toucans roamed around near this temple. The stelae in the area were full of carvings. The carvings on many of them were visible only in direct sunlight—visitors making rubbings of carvings have worn them down.

In the nearby museum, the bones of the man from the tomb in Temple I were laid out with the beautiful jade jewelry with which he was buried—a painted vase depicting a Maya figure smoking a cigarette stands nearby.

At the Central Acropolis, I sat on the stone throne above the porch of nine doors where the high priest watched the games in a ball court below. I looked across the Plaza with Temple I and II at either end. Several excavated palaces lay beyond the temple—truly a fascinating place. (Tikal was shown in the movie *Star Wars*.)

Late afternoon, we checked into the Jaguar Inn near the airport—our honeymoon destination. At dinner, we met a young lady from Merida, Mexico. She was dining with a retired commercial pilot who was teaching her to fly a twin-engine plane. Another lady about our age visiting from the States joined us. The conversation led to a discussion about the ruins. The gates to the ruins close in late afternoon—they all arrived after the gates closed. The young girl really wanted to see the ruins right away.

"I wish I had been here in time to see them today. I'm studying anthropology and can't wait to see them."

Terry said: "There's a full moon tonight. Maybe we can talk a couple of the guides into taking us to the Plaza tonight."

"That sounds great."

The guides agreed and obtained permission from the guards who, with rifles in tow, took us there in their vehicle. The temples and buildings were transformed in the moonlight—ethereal. Once again sitting on the throne of the high priest, I felt that at any moment I would see the Mayans moving about in the courtyard.

The young girl was so alive with interest in the place. I watched as she trotted up the steps of Temple II. The steps are very narrow—she ran diagonally back and forth as the Indians did in the past. This certainly was a memorable ending to our visit to Tikal.

After spending the night at the Jaguar Inn, we were off the ground and heading for El Estor at 6:15. A cloud cover prevented any sightseeing now. Terry found a hole in the clouds, circled down through it, and came to the runway of the airport at the plant site at El Estor—we were in time for Mass.

Monday morning we took off from the airport heading for Aurora Airport in Guatemala City. Our final destination on this flight was Playa Samara on the Nicoyan Peninsula of Costa Rica.

Touching down at the airport, the plane was fueled and the flight plan filed for our trip to San Jose, Costa Rica. Taking off at noon, we headed southeast-east from Aurora Airport, elevation 5,000 feet, with full tanks and baggage. That necessitated a very slow climb-out.

"We'll really have to take it easy so the stall warning doesn't sound off."

"I think I'll keep looking around for possible emergency landing spots—I see that ridge ahead that we'll need to clear."

"We'll make it okay—there's no place to land here over the city anyway."

I looked around; he was right: all I saw were houses and buildings and soccer fields full of players.

We made the ridge and we were home free—to the left, a volcano put forth a column of steam like some giant factory. Soon the voice on the radio asked us to identify ourselves: we were flying over the country of El Salvador. There were many, many farms under cultivation in that tiny country. The Coco River came into view. It flowed through the jungle to the Gulf of Fonseca—the river separated a little sliver of Honduras from El Salvador on the Pacific Coast.

"That's the Gulf of Fonseca ahead so we'll be flying over water for a while now."

"Yeah, I see on the chart we'll come ashore when we reach Nicaragua."

"We'll need to refuel in Managua."

"I feel better over land even though we won't lose sight of land flying over the Gulf."

Crossing a section of the Gulf, we saw volcanic islands poking their heads out of the water. We reached the shore of Nicaragua—Lake Managua soon passed below us. As we neared Managua, we looked down a volcanic crater with a lake of the greenest water ever seen and right alongside it, another crater with a lake of the bluest water ever seen.

We landed at Las Mercedes Airport in Managua, three hours and fifteen minutes after take-off from Guatemala. The terminal was locked for siesta time—we needed to find restrooms post haste. We gained access to the terminal through the plastic curtain on the baggage ramp—any port in a storm. We crawled up the ramp, through the serrated curtain and into the terminal. No one seemed to notice us as we made our way to the restrooms—the men inside were engrossed in a game of checkers.

When siesta time was over; our papers were checked, the plane received fuel and we were on our way again. (It was May Day so the charge was double for the services—the people were not supposed to be working.)

"There's Lake Nicaragua coming up—that's a really large lake."

"According to the chart, it has two islands in it."

"Look, that first island crater is puffing steam like crazy—it's a cooling volcano."

"Wow, that's awesome."

Soon the stark rigid lines of the mountains we were seeing gave way to softer rolling mountains and we were in Costa Rica. Coming down the valley to San Jose is always a thrilling experience. We landed at Tobias Bolanus International Airport just twenty minutes before they closed down for the night.

Customs were again cleared and we were on our way to Avenida Central and Hotel Plaza. The first persons we saw at the hotel were our old friends Jose Alvarez and his wife (he was the Cat representative for Costa Rica—we knew him in Peoria).

I was gone the minute my head hit the pillow that night. At breakfast the next morning, we met one of the maids we had known before when we lived here. After lunch, shared with Jose, we were off the ground heading for our final destination: Samara Beach.

As we flew, Puntarenas on the Gulf of Nicoya came into view; that brought back memories of living there for a short time back in the '60s. Our road-building equipment and our home-goods shipment came through the port of Puntarenas.

Up ahead now, we could see the beautiful white sand beaches on the Pacific shoreline of the Nicoyan Peninsula—Samara was the queen of them all. The tide was out making it possible for us to land on the beach right in front of Carmen's *pension*. This was a dream come true for me, heading for the beach with Terry at the controls—this was his first visit in ten years. It was still the same large gorgeous stretch of white sand beach curving out to the rocky point in the distance.

Carmen and Nicolas welcomed us with open arms. A few changes were made since our last visit—little cabins were added to the rooms that were part of the original *pension*. We chose the Matrimonia cabin—*cama doble con bano*.

After unloading the plane, Terry flew the plane to the cement runway a short distance away. (That runway was built when the children and I visited Samara when we lived in Suriname.) It didn't take long to assume the nice slow pace of life at Samara. Days of walking on the beach, walking out on the reef, swimming in the blue, blue ocean, smelling a wood fire and knowing Carmen was cooking up more black beans and rice and tortillas—it was just exactly what we needed—another exotic honeymoon.

When Nicholas needed to get supplies from Nicoya, Terry flew him there—a nice break from the long bus ride it ordinarily took for that chore. Saturday, we flew to Nicoya. We approached the dirt runway of the airport—below us lay the house we lived in back in the '60s. It's just a short distance from the end of the runway. That brought back memories of hearing the planes come over our house then. (The children climbed the big tree in the backyard, sat on the large branch in direct line with the runway and pretended they were piloting the plane coming in.) A short walk from the airport, over the river, past the saw mill brought us to Hotel Ali. We called home from there—all was well on the home front. In the morning, we went to Mass at the local church in the plaza across the street from the hotel.

While in Nicoya, we visited Jose, Terry's godchild—he was born to Avelina who did our washing when we lived there. Jose accompanied us to Samara. The few days spent together there, he never left Terry's side—if Terry went swimming, Jose went swimming, if Terry dove under a wave, Jose dove under a wave. If Terry stood up and put his hands on his hips, Jose put his hands on his hips—sure looked cute.

A couple of days before our departure, a Gringo, Dave Casady, saw us at Carmen's.

"It's been a long time since I've talked to an American—what's all the latest?"

After a lengthy conversation he said: "I would like you to come and meet my wife and have dinner with us. I'll bring you back after dinner."

"That's sounds good to me, how about you, Mother?"

"Okay, I'll tell Carmen we won't be here for dinner."

I went inside to look for Carmen. When I told her of our plans, she was very upset.

"Please don't go with him—he's a bad man. I don't want you to go."

I motioned Terry to come over. Carmen repeated her concern about our plans.

"Carmen, I don't see any cause for alarm—he'll bring us back after dinner."

We climbed into his waiting Jeep and drove off across the beach to the next cove, Carillo Beach. His first stop there was at a bar where Dave bought a large amount of liquor. I began to feel very uneasy.

From there we took a road up the nearby mountain. His house was situated atop this mountain—he owned 2,500 acres there. The house was luxurious. From it, 1,200 feet up, we could see five bays of the ocean.

His wife met us at the door—inside, the custom-made furniture made the rooms picture-perfect. However, there were no preparations for a meal being made; his wife apparently was on a liquid diet of cocktails and soon Dave helped her to her bedroom.

Dave rejoined us. "Please excuse her, alcohol is a problem for her now—when we lived in the States she was very athletic and received trophies in sailing competition in Maine."

He brought some shrimp cocktail from the kitchen to the low table in the living room. As we ate, the story unfolded. He had taken off with all the retirement money from some union funds in the States to live in Costa Rica where they couldn't touch him. I really wanted to leave! There was no one preparing dinner so Terry said: "I think we'd better get back to Carmen's"

"It's getting dark, you can stay the night and I'll take you back in the morning."

"We'd rather go now."

"No, we have a room for you; the maid will come in the morning and cook breakfast for us."

We reluctantly spent the night there with Dave and his wife, their pet turkey, Sylvester, who patrolled the patio by our bedroom, their toad, Eduardo, and an unnamed iguana. As Dave bade us "good night," he told us there were surveillance cameras on the road to the house and around the house. He asked us not to make any unusual loud noises because he slept with a gun nearby—what a way to live! We should have listened to Carmen!

Breakfast was served by their maid in the morning—this time he did keep his word and drove us back to the *pension*. Terry told him we'd fly over their house the next morning and wag our wings on the way out.

As we approached the *pension*, Carmen came running out to meet us.

"I didn't sleep all night; I was so afraid I'd never see you again."

I hugged her tightly. "I didn't think we'd get back either; it's so good to see you."

The next morning we loaded up the plane, took off and flew over the house on the mountain, wagged the wings and with the compass showing the reciprocal of the trip down, headed back to San Jose across the Gulf of Nicoya. We spent that night with Jose Alvarez and his family.

In the morning, we were off again on our way to Managua, Nicaragua. It was a very clear day. In Lake Nicaragua, a large cluster of tiny islands were visible—most of them just large enough for the house and dock on them.

In Managua, we fueled the plane—it's less than one hundred feet above sea level there, it's very hot and it seemed a long time before we reached our altitude of 9,500 feet. This time we flew over the Pacific end of the Gulf of Fonseca. Facing the sun this time, I was busy keeping Terry and myself awake. The warmth of the sun and the sound of the engine were very conducive to sleep.

"Watch for that river that flows into the Gulf."

"Okay, I'll do that."

We made land just where the chart said we should: at the Coco River by Honduras. From there, we dodged large cloud build-ups across El Salvador to Guatemala City—like flying between huge white canyon walls.

Back in Guatemala City, we topped off our last evening together with dinner at the St. Charles Restaurant. As we finished dinner, the waiter rolled a cart to our table. On the cart was a bottle of propane gas with a heating tip, a striker lighter, a pot of coffee, two Irish coffee glasses, brandy, Kahlua, a dish of whipped cream, a container of cinnamon, sliced lemon, a small dish of sugar and a strange-looking object. Four metal saucers, at intervals of about six inches, were attached at a tilted angle to a two-foot metal stand. Each saucer had a small slit cut into the bottom end of the tilted angle.

The waiter took one of the glasses, wiped the rim of it with a slice of lemon, turned the glass upside down into the dish of sugar, burnt the sugar on the rim with the propane torch, again rubbed the edge of the glass in the sugar and placed it below the bottom saucer of the stand. An ounce each of brandy and Kahlua were poured into a metal container. The lights in the restaurant dimmed as the waiter heated the metal container with the torch until it flamed, poured the flaming liquid into the top saucer: as the liquid cascaded down through the slits of the remaining saucers, cinnamon was sprinkled above the liquid sending off glittering sparks until it drained into the glass below. An equal amount of coffee was then added to the glass. Whipped cream, sprinkled with a little more cinnamon, topped off the drink—their version of Irish coffee. The lemony-sugar taste on the rim blended in as the coffee was sipped—it was fantastic!

Two of the secretaries from Guatemala, Sandra and Sylvia, came to visit us later in the States. They brought along a coffee maker like the one described above which someone in Guatemala had manufactured for them. The highlight at the close of our special family gatherings now, is serving St. Charles Restaurant Irish Coffee. The grandchildren are designated the jobs of turning off the lights at the proper time and sprinkling the cinnamon on the liquid. On one occasion, the Irish pastor of our parish, while watching the procedure, remarked: "No Irishman would wait that long for a drink."

The next morning, I was off to the States, Terry was off to El Estor for another two months of work—what a honeymoon this was!

Bob, Sean, Christopher, Brigid, Hilary and Camille had things running smoothly upon my return to Elmwood. So life went on. Sean had his calves to raise—he bought them when they were about a week old and we slaughtered them when they were about a year old. We always had veal in the freezer. Bob left during this time to take a job with Beech Aerospace in Jackson, Mississippi.

Terry finished his work with International Nickel in 1978—he sold the plane in Guatemala. From there he went to Venezuela in answer to a request by Vinccler C.A., regarding possible work there. Subsequently, he had several short-term contracts with them

One day our son Robert called from his apartment in Athens, Greece. He now made his home there working for Beech Aerospace—he did electronic maintenance work on C-12's used by the Army in the Near and Middle East: BASI had contracts with the Army.
"How about visiting me here, Mom—I'll pick up the tab?"
I was speechless for a while.
"Are you still there, Mom?"
"Yes, I'm just thinking about what you said. I'll…I'll get back with you."
Mmm, I'll never get another chance like this—maybe I should go for it. Little did I know at that time, how much more travel some of our children would provide for me.

After talking over the new development with Terry and the children, I decided to take up Bob's offer. A friend of ours, Josie McGowan, told me her son had a travel agency and could give me information on getting to Greece for the least amount of money—I wanted to take it easy on Bob.

Thus began another phase of my life: seeing new parts of the world through my children.

Mr. McGowan scheduled me on a tour to Athens from LaGuardia in New York for just the price of the air fare since I'd be living with Bob. I found later this was not the best idea.

I left Peoria on a flight to LaGuardia via Chicago and arrived there early afternoon. Our flight to Athens was scheduled to depart at 4:00 p.m. The departure time kept changing—5:00, 6:00, 7:00 p.m. The people at the counter finally told what was happening. All the people did not show for the tour so they were calling people on the waiting list to try and fill the plane. There was no way I could reach Bob to let him know this.

About 11:00 p.m., we finally took off. The ocean looked black as we left shore with just a few lights from ships. As dawn broke, there was a thick layer of clouds below. Then, suddenly, I saw a column of beautiful pink clouds, rising from the gray clouds below, which caught the rays of the rising sun—such beauty seen only by us on the plane—God really spoils us.

We approached the airport at Athens through mounds of billowy sunlit clouds. As we landed, the crew gave the usual instructions to remain seated until the plane stopped. Many on board ignored this and began standing in the aisle, anxious to get off the plane. The stewardess pleaded with them to get back to their seats to no avail.

"Okay, you're on your own—we take no responsibility for any injuries."

Before she actually finished the announcement, the plane suddenly stopped and like dominos, they all went down—she completely ignored them.

Bob had checked with the airport periodically on the status of my flight and arrived shortly after I did. He took me to his home—the first floor of a large house which was in walking distance of the beach. I really enjoyed that.

The beach on the Aegean Sea was so elegant—tall willowy plants welcomed you to the white sand beach. A sculpted platform in the deeper water provided the drop-off for the swimmers. Huge yachts lay at anchor in the distance adding a pleasing backdrop to the scene.

On one Sunday, the Catholic community of the English-speaking people had a picnic on a reserved section of the beach: it began with the celebration of the Mass.

Pontoon boats with a foot-powered paddle wheel were available—Bob decided we'd use one to get a closer look at the yachts. It took a lot of paddling. I became a little squeamish as we approached the yachts and saw the water was so deep it actually looked black. On the return trip, my job was making sure the bow of the boat kept pointing to the home spot on the beach while Bob paddled. I was a happy sailor when we made shore.

I learned to shop for local food items in the shops nearby and did some cooking. I also felt quite elegant washing dishes in the marble sink in the kitchen—where else would you find marble used for that?

Seeing the Acropolis for the first time, rising above the city as we drove along the crowded city street below, took my breath away. Later, as we walked through the beautiful ruins of the temples, I was deeply moved when standing at the spot where St. Paul preached to the Greeks about the one true God. He was surrounded by the majesty of all the temples of the Greek gods rising above him—it is an awesome feeling!

The area around the temples has open-air theaters which are still used for various theatrical productions.

That evening, we ate dinner in a restaurant that afforded a beautiful view of the Acropolis. As it grew dark, the Acropolis suddenly began to come alive in color and music—we watched in awe as the "Light Show" displayed the fine architecture of the temples and buildings in dancing colors enhanced by the sound of the music. What an ending to a memorable day!

During my stay in Athens, I was reminded of the fact that St. Thecla was a Greek convert of St. Paul—he called her his apostle because she helped him when he preached in Athens. When Bob introduced me to some of the local people, they were very familiar with my name—here in the States, hardly anybody has ever heard it.

Bob was called to repair a plane in Vicenza, Italy, one day so I went with him. Our first stop was Rome, Italy. He always carried a bag with him with the tools of his trade and all his necessary papers in case he needed to leave the country in a hurry—his "bug-out bag."

As we went through surveillance before boarding the continuing flight to Vicenza, they pulled him out of line and brought him to the back office and made him explain what each tool did. We barely made the continuing flight in time.

In Vicenza, we spent time with Tom Watson and his wife—Tom was an American who worked for BASI there. On one occasion, we visited an old castle. After completing the tour, we returned to our car in the parking lot and found someone had parked their car behind ours — there was no way to get out. Luckily, it was a small car; Tom and Bob picked up the rear end of it and moved it aside, then did the same to the front end to give us room to leave. This brought on much yelling and gesturing on the part of some people standing by the castle at a higher level above—they thought we were stealing the car. Calm returned as we got into our car and proceeded on our way.

Driving to Venice one day, I learned there is no speed limit on the highway in Italy. I felt a little whip of the car and saw a sports car disappearing on the highway ahead of us. I couldn't guesstimate his speed.

In Venice we fed pigeons in St. Mark's Square, toured the palace, walked across the Bridge of Tears associated with the prison there. When we ate lunch at a restaurant, seeing the price of the items, I could identify with the Merchant of Venice and his "pound of flesh."

As we prepared to leave Vicenza on our return trip to Athens, Bob said: "Mom, here at security, you take my bag and I'll take yours. Maybe we'll get lucky and get through quickly."

"What if they take me to the back room—how will I explain the tools?"

"We'll deal with that when it happens."

"Okay, we'll try it."

I laid his bag down on the table. They didn't even touch it and sent me on my way. Bob laid down my bag—they looked at him, opened the bag and spread everything out on the table—he must just look suspicious.

As we were preparing to land in Rome, Bob said: "Mom, I don't want to go through that mess again. They don't have a jetway here so instead of getting on the shuttle to the terminal, we'll get off the plane, go up through the landscaped part by the parking lot at the entrance and come in through the front door as though we've been in Rome and just came in for our flight to Athens."

"What if the security people see us? I remember seeing the military in the terminal with guns when we came through before."

"It's worth a try."

"I don't know about that, Bob."

"We'll be okay."

We left the plane, casually walked across the tarmac toward the front of the terminal. We came to a landscaped part between the runway and the parking lot.

"Bob, this is too steep an incline for me to get up."

"Come on."

I continued struggling.

"I have to use my hands to help me up this incline."

(In other words, I had to crawl—he, of course, had the bags.)

He looked down at me from his level.

"If anyone asks me, I'll tell them I don't know that old lady following me."

I made it and together we walked through the front entrance to the flight leaving for Athens.

By the way, I've never been in Rome since.

One afternoon, we were getting out of the car in front of Bob's house after an afternoon of sightseeing, when we heard a voice from the front porch.

"It's about time you came home."

We stopped dead in our tracks.

That sounds like my husband, Terry. How can that be? I must be hallucinating.

I looked up and there was Terry sitting on the front porch. Recovering from the shock, we ran to meet him and to hear the story behind this.

"After you left Elmwood, I received an offer to go to Indonesia on a short-term contract with World Bank and the government of Indonesia for their Transmigration number 2."

"In what capacity?"

"As a consultant along with a man from Australia and a Frenchman from Africa—the government of Indonesia is relocating some of their people from the main islands to the many other uninhabited smaller islands. They need help in determining how best to clear the land."

"So you decided to stop here on your way to Indonesia."

"That's it."

"Well, you certainly did a good job of surprising us."

That evening as we ate dinner at a restaurant, it began to rain—a real cloudburst. We were soaked before we made it to Bob's little compact car. As we turned on to the ocean-front street to his house, the car began floating.

Terry and Bob got out of the car and began guiding it while instructing me on the use of the steering wheel as a rudder. Apparently, the heavy rain flowed unobstructed down to the ocean and flooded the street on the way. That was my first ride in a floating car—Terry and Bob's easiest job of pushing a car.

We enjoyed a few days of sightseeing together before Terry left. I followed later on my return trip home. It proved to be an incredible trip—it was the tour plane again and passengers with families disposed of the baby food jars, napkins, diapers into the aisles. It was impossible to walk safely down the aisles. The crew asked them to put all of it into bags they provided but none did that. Then the captain made an announcement.

"We are going to land in Paris—everyone will leave the plane as best you can. You will be locked into a room at the airport until a maintenance crew completely cleans out the plane."

That was my first and only visit ever to Paris—I did see the Eiffel Tower though as we descended to the airport. The extra time for all of this made it necessary to stay a night in a hotel at the airport in New York before continuing on to Elmwood.

Chapter XI

More New Worlds

At home, everyone was doing fine—it was so good to see all of them again. Besides Sean, Christopher, Brigid, Hilary and Camille, there were Kevin, Micki and our first grandchild, Carmen—she had grown so much while I was gone.

Later, I walked toward the barnyard. Sean's calf looked up as I called his name—he was quite attached to me before I left. Now, he showed his disapproval of my absence by turning his head away.

"Bubbles, don't you remember me?"

He ignored me until I was at the fence, when he finally walked very slowly toward me—then began licking my outstretched hand. We were friends again.

The winters in Elmwood were getting to us—the wind blowing across the prairie was awesome. Terry took a trip to the southwest to check out cities more winter-friendly. When he returned, Tucson was the city he chose.

The summer of 1979, I took off for Tucson to find a house to rent. I stopped in Missouri to visit my folks, then off to Tulsa, Oklahoma, where the newlyweds, Rory and Amy, were living, then to Amarillo, Texas, where the other newlyweds, Terry Jr. and Sue, were living (both Rory and Terry were married in May of that year—Rory and Amy in Missouri, Terry and Sue in Texas).

In New Mexico, I felt a twinge of homesickness when I saw a family with young children enjoying a meal in a restaurant—brought back many memories. Coming down the mountain from Ruidoso, I was delighted to see a young Indian boy riding a horse on a dirt road parallel to the highway—his hair flying in the wind, he was able to keep up with me for a little while. I spent the night in Alamogordo. I left a call for 3:00 a.m. at the desk—the AC in the car wasn't working too well so I didn't relish crossing the White Sands too late in the day.

It was cool as I started out the next morning and a pleasant trip down Highway 70 to I-10 at Las Cruces. From there on I got the real taste of the desert—this would take some "getting used to."

My final destination was the YWCA in Tucson. I lived there while working for Kelly Services—after work, I checked out homes to rent. I found what I wanted on the south side of Tucson near Tucson International Airport. I set up housekeeping with the few articles I had with me and waited for Terry, Brigid, Hilary and Camille to come with our belongings (Chris was on the wheat harvest crew and joined us before school started).

Terry went on another very short-term contract with World Bank/ Indonesia before signing a six-month contract in 1983 to work in Santo Domingo, Dominican Republic—I accompanied him there.

The company provided us with a hotel-apartment so I could cook our meals. We thoroughly enjoyed our time there. On weekends, we explored the beautiful old part of the city on the waterfront—the home of Diego Colon, the son of Columbus, was our favorite. The doorways to some parts of the home indicated that the family was of much smaller stature than us. I loved the courtyards of the museums with the large candelabra holding the huge candles lighting the area.

The beaches on the northern side of the island were also inviting. Traveling through the small towns as we went north, baseball fields in each of them were always filled with players and fans. They really love baseball.

We attended an English Mass offered periodically for the English-speaking residents. A group there raised money for Mother Teresa's nuns who cared for abandoned infants. The group decided we needed to raise money to buy a freezer so the nuns could keep larger amounts of food on hand.

After one of those Masses, I spoke with the lady who bought the food and brought it to the nuns.

"May I go with you when you go this time?"

"You certainly may—I'll pick you up in the morning. I just want to let you know that the nuns warned me about the diseases I am exposed to when visiting them. As a precaution, I was told to take off all my clothes when I returned home, put them in the washer and take a good shower. That's something we must always do."

"I will do that."

The next morning we bought the food and were on our way. I was introduced to another part of the Dominican Republic. As we approached the building, it stood out like a sore thumb among all the other ones around it—it was sparkling clean.

Nun with children at the Children's Center

Inside, one part of the house was filled with little baby beds, some with very sick little babies in them—in another part, recovering children were playing with toys. On the patio, little ones were sitting on potties as they were potty-trained. Everything, everywhere, was painted and clean.

When we opened the refrigerator, there was just a little milk left in a container there—nothing else. We filled the refrigerator with the perishable items. As we opened the pantry door, the same was true there—only a few cans remained. As we finished storing the food, we approached one of the nuns.

"Our parishioners want to get you a freezer so you can store more food to make sure you always have enough."

"Thank you for the thought but God always provides for us—see, you filled the refrigerator and gave us other food when we needed it: we always have enough."

We went in to visit the sick children in their beds—I saw with my own eyes children who were starving. I went to the bed of a little girl found on the street the day before. She didn't have any desire to eat or drink anymore. A nun stood by the bed, trying different ways to get some liquid into her—the girl finally let her trickle a little cola down her throat from a spoon. Sister asked me to continue to do that for her—I was so happy she kept swallowing the cola. When I left with my friend later that day, the little girl was still drinking by the spoonful. A couple of weeks later, when we visited her, she was eating and drinking and beginning to get her colored pigmentation back in her skin.

Terry and I visited them shortly before we left Santo Domingo. One of the nuns told us to come with her. She took us across the side street to the house that served as their convent.

"I want you to visit my special friend before you leave."

She took us into the room serving as a chapel and pointed to her Friend. It was Jesus in the small wooden tabernacle sitting on the altar. We knelt down together and visited with her Friend.

A few days before we left Santo Domingo, with our passports in my purse, I went downtown to get cash and travelers checks—I used the usual mode of transportation, the *collectivo*, a taxi of sorts. We were told it was the safe way to go but to make sure they were the right ones. The "right ones" were cars with damaged parts that were replaced with all sorts of parts from different cars and had a bright array of colors: a fender from a red car, the door from a yellow car, a hood from a green car, etc. Those owning them picked up people standing on the corners until the car was full and then deposited them wherever needed.

After finishing my business that particular day, I waited on a corner for a collective. I don't know why I didn't notice that the car that stopped was not a *collectivo*—it was all one color—I just wasn't thinking. A male passenger was sitting in the back seat—I went to the back door of the car, the man got out, pushed me into the middle of the front seat and we took off.

"Let me out at this corner!"

We kept going.

I was terrified—an American woman had been robbed and raped just recently.

"Let me out now," I shouted as I jabbed my elbows into the sides of the two men.

The car stopped; I dug my heels into the man's foot as I jumped out. I ran the rest of the way to the apartment. When I was inside, I fell down on my knees and thanked my guardian angel for protecting me.

When I looked inside my purse, my billfold was gone but, thank God, our passports were there.

Not a very pleasant way to end our stay.

In 1984, Terry contracted with Green Construction Company to train operators and mechanics of heavy equipment for one year at Guymine, a bauxite mine in Guyana, South America.

A Canadian company had been mining bauxite there but the government wanted to nationalize them so they could do the mining themselves; that didn't work out so they hired Green Construction, located in Iowa, to restart the mine in Linden, Guyana.

I joined Terry a little later—some of the wives and I flew down in the company's corporate jet. Guyana is the only country I lived in where I marked off the days with an X on the calendar. Praying the Liturgy of the Hours every day helped a lot though—we knew we prayed in communion with our Secular Franciscan brothers and sisters. Virginia Moreno in our Fraternity in Tucson faithfully sent the newsletter which kept us in touch with our spiritual family—that supplemented our family's letters, cards and phone calls..

We lived in an apartment building specified for the families of foreign employees. The American supervisor of the project wanted only men on bachelor status there—he was not happy with wives and children living in the apartment complex. He and several other employees had their "camp girls," as they were called, living with them in their apartment. Terry and I reminded him that Green Construction said these were family apartments: many of the families had children with them. We didn't think it was a good situation. He disagreed and things remained the same.

One morning, Ismay, who cleaned the apartment and washed the clothes, took the key to the door of our laundry room located in the hall outside our kitchen door, to start the washing. (The room was used only by us.) In a few seconds, she came screaming into the living room, quite hysterical. I sat her down and tried to find out what happened. She motioned me to the laundry room; I went in and there at the entrance was a bowl with urine in it—it smelled quite strongly. How could it have gotten there when the door was always locked and we supposedly had the only key?

I picked up the bowl and came through the kitchen on the way to the bathroom. When she saw me with the bowl in my hand, she became hysterical again: I flushed it down the toilet and came back to her. She was still terrified.

"That urine is the sign that someone has put a hex on you—they have much power because they got into your locked room."

"Ismay, my belief in God and His protection of me is much stronger than that witch's hex."

"No, no, I've seen what happens to people that have a hex put on them."

"Ismay, I'll be all right."

I went toward the front door of our apartment ready to take my usual walk through the whole housing complex, Richmond Hill, which was quite large; some were individual houses—Ismay begged me not to go. When she saw I was going anyway, she held me back.

"Let me go first and look."

She cautiously opened the front door, checked all around the entryway and did the same thing at the outside door.

"The next thing the witch will do is put a poisonous snake somewhere. I wanted to make sure there was not one outside the doors."

I took my walk, stopped and visited some friends along the way and came home. Ismay was still sitting in the living room and jumped up to hug me when she saw me coming. She was much too shaken to work; I told her she could stay if she wanted but could go home for the day if she wished: she went home.

Ismay came back the next day but was very cautious. She apparently learned that the girl living with the man in the apartment above us was the one who ordered the hex put on me. The girl objected to our wishes to have only families living there. However, no further similar incidents occurred.

(We knew that the man who lived in that apartment was from Tucson: Months after we returned home, I was at the airport waiting for my relatives to come in. As I watched those deplaning from another flight, the man from the apartment in Guyana came walking out, behind him came the girl he lived with there but how differently she appeared. She always looked disdainfully at me when she saw me in Guyana: now, she glanced at me, put her head down and walked on, quite far behind the man. How my heart went out to her!)

The yards around the apartment buildings were full of tall thick weeds. I longed to see some sort of landscaping transform them. I ventured into the weeds in the section by our front door one day and found stones arranged to form flower beds beneath all the weeds. I told Terry about them when he came home.

"I'll find out who we can hire to cut down the weeds and see what we find below."

"That'll be great—maybe we'll have a nice place for me to sit and work on my quilt."

"It's a good thing you brought what you needed for that quilt. The twelve-hour days, six days a week doesn't leave much time for us, does it?"

"That's for sure. I'm so glad I brought it along. Amy's grandmother recommended this design, called 'cathedral window' with the small squares. I can hand-sew the small squares and then sew the squares together as I go along."

"You really needed something like this to fill your days. Not having a car and no license if you did have a car, makes it pretty rough."

"I really enjoy working on it. It's fun too using scraps of material from the clothes Sue sewed for Sarah and Rebekah—I remember seeing the girls wearing the dresses at home."

"I'm glad we can at least drive around on Sunday and see a little bit of the country."

"I really enjoy those rides—I'd never seen so many different kinds of orchids on trees in the jungle before—they're breathtaking."

"We're able to see a few of the little surrounding villages too."

The quilt was large enough for the top of a queen-size bed when we returned home—it still had some unfinished squares. I folded it and displayed it on the top of my cedar chest. This past summer I gave it to Camille, who makes quilts. She's finishing it for her bed.

Terry found a young man with a machete; he cut down all the weeds; flower beds arranged with different-sized rocks were revealed. I collected seeds and bulbs from the local people living in our complex—they all had beautiful flower gardens and were happy to share with me. I didn't try growing orchids though—Yvonne had a beautiful variety of them. There was also plenty of room for chairs among the flower beds. I spent many hours sewing there in the garden. It became a gathering place for the neighbors too. The families periodically had potluck dinners together in their homes—the garden was a spot for those gatherings after that.

Then a colony of ants decided to share the garden with me. They were militantly stripping all the flowers and leaves from one section of a flower bed—only stalks remained. I followed them across the road to a large entrance to their home. I dusted the hole with Sevin powder and thought that would take care of it.

The next morning, however, they were making great strides in eliminating another section. Ismay and her friend, who worked in the apartment next door, joined me tracking them to the same hole. Her friend said: "The ants here have college degrees and know how to handle the poison—see they have another hole and are walking alongside your powder."

"I'll just have to find something better and stronger."

Terry brought home some liquid exterminator the next day—I poured that down the hole and I didn't see them anymore.

This was the first time we lived in a country under Socialist/Communist rule. The government leaders spoke on the radio about how great the country was.

However, the grocery stores had empty shelves, wheat or wheat products were forbidden to be imported into the country—they were only available on the black market.

If a store had milk or dairy products, long lines of people formed trying to buy them. The lack of these products took a tremendous toll on the children. Green Construction had everything available for us in the commissary so I shared the milk products Terry and I received with the families with children living in our housing complex.

One day a young man, a member of the local army, came by as he patrolled the housing complex. He sat down alongside me in the garden. Soon he was telling me how much better their type of government was than the government in the United States.

"Sir, you obviously have no difficulty in getting all the food and clothing you want. Doesn't it bother you that the hospital has so many children suffering from malnutrition in it because the people can't buy milk and cheese and food they need for them?"

"Not really—I get what I need."

"And that's because you work for the government."

The conversation ended there and he went on his way.

(Terry told me it would be better if I refrained from conversations like that in the future.)

One of the friends I visited on my walks was Yvonne Hinds. Her husband, Sam, was a chemist at Guymine where Terry worked—he tested oil samples for Terry.

Five years after we left, in 1990, Sam was active in the Guyanese Action for Reform and Democracy preparing the Guyanese people for a more democratic society. He was appointed to the post of prime minister following the victory in the 1992 elections and on the death of President Jagan became Guyana's interim president. He is prime minister now and we still receive a Christmas card from Sam and Yvonne every year.)

An invitation to spend a few days on the island of Barbados was gratefully received by the wives—executives of Green Construction were coming to Guyana for a meeting with the local company. They didn't want to leave the corporate jet on the ground in Georgetown for the duration of the meeting—they chose to fly the plane back to Barbados in the interim.

It was a wonderful break from the daily routine. Since it was necessary to stay at a hotel near the airport so we would be available at any time, we didn't get to the beach but we thoroughly enjoyed the holiday.

Terry and I went to Mass at St. Joseph the Worker Church where Father Patrick Connors, S.J., was pastor. He and his assistant, Father George Vanderwood, S.J., a Guyanese priest, also served missions located in the interior. They were at best tolerated by the local government. Father Connors was expelled from the missions in the interior in 1980 because of his influence with the people there.

The Communion hosts, made of wheat, used at the Consecration of the Mass were illegal—we actually broke the law when we received Holy Communion. The local people had such strong Faith despite the opposition of the government—they were wonderful examples for us. We loved their singing during the Masses. Father George, a great guitarist, had a musical group of the youth in the parish—we enjoyed watching them perform.

Father Connors and Father George came to our home for dinner at times—it was so neat to see how much they enjoyed the cheese, milk and meat that we were able to offer them.

Shortly after we left Guyana, Bishop Singh along with other civic leaders denounced the 1985 election results: the government in retaliation against the Church, deported Father Connors, with no reasons given. He had given many years of service to the country. Fr. Andrew Morrison, S.J., wrote about this in his book *Justice—The Struggle for Democracy in Guyana 1952–1992* (ISBN: 976-8157-52-6).

Father Connors served in various parishes on islands in the Caribbean after that until he returned to Guyana. We kept in touch with him through the "Jesuit Missions Newsletters" during that time. He is now in Liverpool, England—Sean visited him recently when United Airlines sent him to England for training on Rolls-Royce engines.

We met Father Chris Corbally, S.J., from England when he visited Linden—we met him again years later here in Tucson when he was with the Vatican Observatory at the University of Arizona.

The company provided a van and driver for the wives for occasional shopping trips into the capital city, Georgetown. This usually included lunch at the hotel. There were no sandy beaches on the ocean here—just muddy ones like those in Suriname. The swimming pool at the hotel was always a welcome sight.

One of the highlights in the city was the beautiful old wooden Sacred Heart Church—the Jesuit residence and the Sacred Heart School stood alongside it.

Thecla in front of Sacred Heart Church

According to the Jesuit & Friends *magazine, a fire destroyed the church, Jesuit residence and Sacred Heart School on Christmas Day in 2004—it was 134 years old at the time. It started when electrical flashing lights in the Nativity crib sparked a fire—none of the parishioners attending Mass were injured.*

Earlier that day the church was crowded, as more than a hundred children performed a Nativity play during the midnight Mass.

Terry and I also had the privilege of meeting Dr. John and Dr. Evelyn Billings—they pioneered a revolutionary church-backed method for couples to avoid or achieve conception called Natural Family Planning. They addressed doctors and nurses at the hospital in Linden and then gave a public presentation at St. Joseph's Church hall.

They accepted our offer to spend the night at our apartment before returning to Georgetown for their flight to Brazil the next day.

They spent six months traveling all over the world to give presentations and six months in their clinic in Melbourne, Australia

The Billings were told before coming to Central and South America that no men would come to the conferences—the men there would be too macho for that. That proved to be untrue: many men did come.

At the end of Terry's contract in 1985, we took the long way home with a stop at the Pan Am Guest House in Trinidad, then on to the island of Margarita where we stayed at the Margarita Concorde Hotel in Porlamar.

Our next stop was Guayana International Hotel overlooking the La Llovizna Falls in Ciudad Guayana-Puerto Ordaz. There we rented a car and drove to the Guri Dam, one of the largest in the world.

Terry wanted me to see the dam. He was a consultant to Consorcio Macagua-Guri and worked with Vinccler, a major company which constructed the earthen part east of the hydroelectric dam—this eastern part was about five miles long. Terry dealt with equipment operator and maintenance training. The size of dam was mind-boggling. It took quite a while for me to get some idea of what had been accomplished.

Its official name is Central Hidroelectrica Simon Bolivar. The construction started in 1963 with the first part concluding in 1978 with a capacity of 2,065 megawatts in ten units which brought the dam to a maximum level of 215 meters above sea level. The final stage, in which Terry took part, concluded in 1986, elevating the level to 272 m a.s.l.—that meant moving a lot of dirt for the earthen part. Ten units of 630 megawatts each was added in this addition.

Thanks to the Guri Dam, Venezuela is a nation where eighty-two percent of its electricity comes from renewable energy like hydroelectric, allowing it to export more oil.

From there we flew to Caracas to visit with Heinz Anwand, who worked closely with Terry on the Guri Dam. Our last stop in South America was Maracaibo to visit Fidel Clerico, co-owner of Vinccler—he invited us to dinner at his hacienda.

From South America, we headed north to Costa Rica—we planned to see Carmen and the little plot of land I bought at Samara years before when we still lived in Elmwood, Illinois.

We rented a car and took the Pan American Highway to Puntarenas, then on to the Nicoyan Peninsula to the town of Nicoya: the same route we always took when we lived in Nicoya.

The town was different now with many cars and trucks on the streets and even a taxi—not the buses and ox carts we had known. We were so sad to learn from a friend in Nicoya that Carmen was dead; her *pension* no longer existed in Samara.

With my papers in hand, we paid a visit to the lawyer in Nicoya who did the paperwork when I purchased the land. He took us to the recorder's office—a search in the records for the date and location of the plot produced nothing—according to them, we owned nothing. I remembered seeing it recorded when I bought it.

With heavy hearts we left Nicoya and took the new highway to Samara. What a difference from the highway we knew when we lived here—no rivers to ford or turnouts to look for if you met a vehicle. This was a year-round road not just a dry-season road. We wondered if the young man Terry trained to operate road-building equipment when we lived here helped to build this new road.

What a change had taken place at Samara! A low-income housing development covered the stretch of beach to the right of the *pension* all the way to the cliff that hid part of the reef—the reef where our children spent so many hours exploring and where Sean cut his foot and frightened me so many years before.

A different pension occupied the spot where Carmen's had stood. A *kiosk* occupied the plot of land I purchased years before. Our only consolation was that the local people were still enjoying their beautiful Samara—no high-rise hotels here.

On our return trip to San Jose, we took a new shorter route from the Nicoyan Peninsula—a ferry now crossed the Tampisque River above the Gulf of Nicoya. It was no longer necessary to travel to Liberia in order to get to Puntarenas.

We continued on our way through Central America to Guatemala to visit the families we came to know when Terry worked at the nickel mine there. Brigid came down from Tucson and joined us for the beautiful Holy Week services in Antigua and Guatemala City.

When Brigid left for her return trip home, we took off for our last stop which was the Shrine of Our Lady of Guadalupe in Mexico City—the Blessed Mother is the Patroness of the Americas and Patroness of the Unborn under that title.

The shrine is spectacular—it honors the appearance of the Blessed Mother to a poor Indian farmer, Juan Diego in 1531—in that appearance, she imprinted an image of herself on his *tilma*. The *tilma* is displayed in the shrine. As you stand on the moving tread to view it, Our Lady's eyes follow you—although the fabric is coarse and rough, it remains in perfect condition.

In the early 1500s, one in five children was killed as a sacrificial offering to the pagan gods of the Aztecs. As a result of this visit of the Mother of God to Juan Diego, the whole region was transformed—where once fear ruled among the Aztecs, thousands lined up to be baptized. Because this was happening, the practice of child sacrifice was all but eradicated.

What a treasure we have next door to us!

That was the last overseas contract that Terry took—he worked locally after that. However, I traveled to other worlds visiting some of our children who worked overseas during the '80s and '90s—I don't know what prompted them to work overseas.

In July of 1986, I was met by our son Chris at the airport in Frankfort, Germany. I was amazed how much he had grown in stature since I last saw him when he worked for Beech Aerospace in Corpus Christi, Texas. I didn't think there was that much of a growth factor when they're in their twenties.

He now worked at Ramstein Air Force Base in Germany—BASI offered him the work there. They were contracted by the Army to maintain C-12's at that base.

Now, as we drove from Frankfort to the little village where he lived, the countryside looked familiar to me—it was so like the towns and countryside where I was raised in Missouri.

He shared a nice old home with another American couple, Jeff and Wendy, who lived on the top floor. I fit into the population with ease as I rode Chris' bike to the stores to buy groceries—in fact, all spoke to me in German and were surprised I was American and did not speak the language.

Wherever we went to Mass, the congregation sang the Mass in harmony. In restaurants, someone in a group started singing and soon everyone was singing in harmony. That reminded me so much of my childhood when there was always a lot of singing in our home in the little town of Washington, Missouri.

Dachau Concentration Camp—I'll never forget our visit there. All the visitors walking with us to the entrance gate fell silent as we entered the camp—that silence continued as we walked through the compound. The foundations of the barracks still stand in mute testimony of the former occupants.

Inside the museum, the stark life-size pictures of the victims look at you. It begins with the political opponents and on to Jehovah's Witnesses, Jews, gypsies, clergymen and all who endangered the security of the state.

Then on to the crematorium—it was so hard to imagine those huge furnaces burning the people. The prevailing wind from the west once kept the smell of burning corpses filling the camp. Bright red flowers now fill the gutters where blood flowed at one time.

At the end of the compound, stands the Monument of Atonement, a round chapel shaped like a gigantic winepress, built of unhewn rocks and crowned with the crown of thorns. Bishop Neuhaeusler, a former prisoner of Dachau, dedicated the chapel on August 5, 1960.

Chris shared his love of kayaking with Jeff so one weekend was spent in Augsburg—a river was diverted there to form what was known as the "ice canal." The man-made canal, constructed for use for the Olympics, supplied all the types of the water's flow found in the natural rivers for kayak competition.

It was a little scary watching Chris and Jeff roll over and pop up again. At one point, a spot called the "washing machine" because the water swirled in a tight circle, Jeff rolled over and took quite a long time to surface again—I couldn't have held my breath that long.

In Garmish, I watched Chris and Jeff, in their kayaks, drop off a high river bank to the river below. Wendy and I then drove downriver to meet them at the end of that run.

The Berlin Wall was still standing in 1986 when I was there—we took a bus tour through Checkpoint Charlie into East Germany. A car with Russian soldiers followed us everywhere. The towns were dark and dismal with box-like high-rise apartment buildings in shades of gray and brown. Only one model of basic cars, all the same color of gray, could be found. However, we were served the best-tasting sauerkraut and sausage when we ate lunch there.

In the small museum at Checkpoint Charlie, there were many mementos of the things people used for their escape over the Wall; one was the hot air balloon sewn by a family who successfully used the balloon for their escape. I still have the white sweatshirt with the Checkpoint Charlie logo on it that I bought at the museum.

For the trip to West Berlin, it was necessary to go through the official headquarters of the U.S. Army, Europe because Chris worked on U.S. Army planes for BASI at Ramstein Air Base. I was given an Identity Document No. US PP No 030608861 on U.S. Movement Orders.

At the gate, we were briefed by the Army regarding our behavior driving through the Soviet Army gate and the East German highway to West Berlin—we were not to stop anywhere along that highway and if we were stopped by anyone, we were to keep the windows up and refuse to speak with anyone.

At the Soviet gate, Chris was required to salute the soldiers and received propaganda booklets about the Soviet Union titled: "People of Great Character," "Soviet Foreign Policy," "What I Saw in Moscow and Leningrad," "Cudgels of Democracy Versus Fighters for Peace" and "The Soviet Union: Facts Problems Appraisals."

I saw the part of the arch in West Germany pointing across East Germany to West Berlin and the other part of the arch there pointing toward West Germany, completing the arch. The two parts stood in remembrance of the Berlin Airlift. When Russia cut off the supply route to West Berlin during the Cold War, the Allies used this air corridor to fly supplies to the people there to keep them alive.

What a difference it was to see West Berlin—beautiful buildings and parks, cars of every color and model. At the hotel, we learned that Herbert von Karajan was conducting the Berlin Philharmonic Orchestra in Beethoven's Ninth Symphony that evening—we tried to purchase tickets but it was sold out. That was hard to accept.

However, on another weekend, we were driving through Munich and saw advertisements for an opera being performed that afternoon. We were told some tickets were available: season tickets of persons not attending this performance were being sold.

I went into the lobby of the Opera House while Chris went below to the ticket office. There wasn't enough time for us to go to the hotel to change clothes before the performance—there I stood in the lobby in my Checkpoint Charlie sweatshirt and watched the ladies in their formal dresses and furs and men in tux make their way inside. I approached the usher.

"My son is waiting in line to get tickets—if he gets them, would you permit us inside dressed like this?"

He was silent for a while.

"Yes, I will—you have a good reason."

Then I saw Chris—his face said it all. The last ticket was sold to the person in front of him.

On our way to the hotel, I saw another advertisement I could hardly believe—Luciano Pavarotti was performing in a concert in the Olympic Stadium in Munich in a few hours!

We found the stadium and Chris purchased two tickets in Block V3, Row 18, Seats 8 and 9—this translated into the highest balcony behind the stage which was on the floor of the stadium. The stadium is huge—every seat was taken.

Emerson Buckley, conductor of the Fort Lauderdale Symphony, was conducting the orchestra which featured Andrea Griminelli, flutist, who studied at the Paris Conservatory and had performed with Pavarotti in the USA.

179

The concert was wonderful—the acoustics were good considering the type of building. Pavarotti slowly turned around as he sang to include all of us in his audience.

I had recently read a book about Pavarotti — in it was the statement that he signed autographs after concerts until every last person was taken care of, no matter how long the line. We found our way down below the floor of the stadium to the dressing rooms. The line was short for the conductor and the flutist—I was one of the last persons in the long line for Pavarotti. He was very gracious as he signed my program.

Chris is a pilot and belonged to the Aero Club at Ramstein Air Base. He received his instrument rating through his Norwegian instructor Dag, who also worked at the base. Before he left for the weekend, Dag invited us to spend a couple of days with him in Norway.

After leaving Ramstein in the Aero Club plane, we stopped in Denmark to refuel. That country is very flat and even looked spotlessly clean from the air. The terminal was immaculate—very impressive.

From there, we flew out across the Strait to the terminal in Oslo, Norway, where Dag met us. After refueling the plane, Dag took over the controls— away we went across some of the most beautiful country I have ever seen— fjords and hills and flowers everywhere!

"There's our cabin down there on that fjord. Hang on now because I'll buzz the house and let my mom know we're here."

A steep turn and down and around we went—I love that feeling. We saw Dag's mom come out of the cabin and wave to us. Dag waved the wings in return.

"We'll fly to the airport and by the time we drive back to the cabin, she'll have gone to our home. She wanted us to have the cabin to ourselves."

A nice fire glowed in the fireplace taking out the bit of a chill in the late afternoon air. The windows to the front of the house overlooking the water invited us out to explore the grounds. A small estuary to the left was home to a family of swans. The father at the time was busy chasing another swan away from his family—what a display of wing span unfolded between the two of them. Water splashed everywhere. Out in the fjord, the man ski-sailing went down with a big splash. It's a good thing he had on a wet suit—I'm sure the water was quite cold.

Dag went down to the small boat tied to the dock.

"I'm going to get us something for dinner. I'll be back shortly. Help yourself to the snack in the kitchen."

He returned with a container of the best shrimp I have ever tasted.

"Where in the world did you get this wonderful shrimp?"

"A fisherman friend of mine lives just a little way down the fjord—he cooks it in sea water in his special way. He shared some with us."

"It's the best I've ever tasted."

After dinner we walked to the little village near the cabin to check out some stores for souvenirs. The Norweigen girls we met everywhere were so beautiful.

Even though it was late in the evening, it wasn't completely dark—sort of an eerie gray where you could still distinguish everything. When we returned to the cabin, I said good night and went upstairs to the bedroom overlooking the fjord. I spent some time just looking out at the scenery in this eerie light. Chris and the rest were talking downstairs.

I finally lay down and fell asleep. I was awakened by the sound of muffled footsteps. *That's probably Chris or someone going to bed.* It continued for a little while and I fell asleep again.

The next morning, I told them about the incident as we ate breakfast.

"We didn't come near your bedroom—your room is by itself at the front of the house."

"But I heard footsteps…"

They looked at each other and Dag said: "I was telling them last night that my mother has heard footsteps. There was an old fisherman who lived in this cabin until he died. Our family let him live here in his old age. My mother thinks he still roams about at night."

"Well, I was never one who believed in that sort of thing—I can't deny though that I did hear something."

It was a wonderful weekend. The swan family was so much fun to watch. They were a beautiful sight as Poppa, Mama, and the babies glided off from the estuary into the deeper water. I picked some of the seaweed by the water and still have them in a vase on the shelf here at home. The return flight to Germany was beautiful—we refueled in Denmark again; the ice cream in the restaurant there was super.

My last trip with Chris was a flight viewing the castles on the Rhine—he tried to have me take over the controls on that flight back to Ramstein. He didn't succeed though—the plane was too fast for me.

Then it was time to head back home to the States. On the return flight home from Germany, the captain said even though it was August we could see ice and snow down below us. I went to the window and there was snow swirling around down on Iceland. I didn't know we flew that far north on our return.

Chris left Germany a while later—he took an assignment from BASI for work in Honduras. It was there that he met the girl who became his wife.

Sean called me one day in the fall of 1992. He was now working for United Airlines in San Francisco. He and Dotty and family lived in Spain for a while when he worked for BASI there—I didn't get to visit him there.

"Mom, United just started flights into Milan, Italy. I can get you a stand-by ticket to go there to visit Bob and Nancy and the family."

Bob and his family moved to Grisignano, Italy, when he accepted an offer to work for BASI there.

"Oh, Sean, that's wonderful—I would love to go. I'll get with Bob to make all the arrangements there."

The trip was scheduled for October 19. Seats were available from Tucson through Chicago and on to Dulles Airport. On the flight to Milan, I was assigned a seat in the businessmen section of the 747. They handed me a pouch with slipper socks, a blindfold, lotion, toothbrush, etc. I really traveled in style on a stand-by ticket.

Bob met me in Milan—we traveled two and a half hours through beautiful countryside to their home in Grisignano. Rob, Caitlin, Joseph and their mommy, Nancy, greeted me on the front steps of the house. It was so good to see them. It was the first time I saw Joseph (he was born in Italy and has a dual birth certificate). They had quite a schedule of places and things for me to see and do while I was there.

The first weekend on the schedule was a 7:00 a.m. train ride to Venice. (They don't give you much time to get on the train—you must be ready to jump when the door opens.) In Venice we went to St. Mark's Square (I had been there years before when Bob was living in Athens). Now, we enjoyed watching Rob and Caitlin chasing the pigeons around the square, trying to catch them.

Rob and Caitlin in St. Mark's Square in Venice

Later, we boarded a water bus to Murano, a small island where the glass works are located—such beautiful things to look at. I have a love of Christmas ornaments and found one I really liked. It had tiny figures of Joseph, with his staff in hand and Mary kneeling beside Jesus in the manger. The figures were glass and were mounted inside a glass ornament—so beautiful.

After lunch, we took a ferryboat from Isle Murano to Isle Burano—there, lacework is featured. In one of the shops, I saw a tablecloth that caught my breath—small circles of linen cloth held together with the most delicate lace comprised the tablecloth with wide lace forming the border.

Nancy asked the shopkeeper to give her the measurements of the tablecloth. "Mom, I know the measurements of your table and this one is perfect. We'll take this one."

"But Nancy, I can't afford to buy that."

"We've been saving up money to get you one of these lace tablecloths—I saw how much you liked it when you looked at it—that's what we're getting for you. You always set a beautiful table on special occasions for the family—now you have a new tablecloth."

That brought tears to my eyes. Now I use it all the time, especially on the holidays when I put cloth the color of the season under it—the colors show beautifully through the lace.

The sun was setting on the Adriatic as we took the ferryboat back to Murano, then again by water bus to Venice. Venice looked beautiful at night with all the lights reflecting on the water. Coming up the canal to the dock, we saw beautiful chandeliers burning in the large homes along the waterfront.

Bob took a week's vacation. We drove to Segno through the Dalamite Mountains, the foothills of the Alps. The Adige River wound back and forth alongside us with castles up on the hills. Before we turned off the highway to reach Segno on the mountainside, there were signs for the Brenner Pass up ahead. From Segno, we saw the snow-capped Alps.

Our destination was the town square by the church where Fr. Eusebius Kino was baptized. He was a Jesuit missionary who founded the San Xavier Mission on the Toho O'odam Indian Reservation here in Tucson.

There is a statue of him on Kino Parkway here in Tucson—an exact replica of it stands on Piazza P. Eusebio F. Kino on Via Arizona in Segno. (Another sign reads "Piazza Padre E. F Chini," their spelling of his name.)

Bob with Joseph, Thecla, Rob and Caitlin by statue of Padre Kino

We enjoyed a picnic lunch in a little mountain park with an absolutely gorgeous view. There was a little coffee bar on the piazza which served the best cappuccino I had during my stay in Italy—I had two of them and was wired-for-sound far into the night.

"Mom, tonight we're going to a 'Hail and Farewell' dinner at Ristorante Farina.

"What in the world kind of a dinner is that, Bob?"

"The commander of the 6th Air Division hosts a dinner for his servicemen and women and the contract people like me who either are arriving or leaving the country."

"That sounds like fun—I'm looking forward to it."

At the dinner, the commander introduced me too since I came into Milan the same day he did. They served a beautiful seven-course dinner.

The next weekend in October, we drove down to Assisi—I was going to see the birthplace of St. Francis, the founder of our order, the Secular Franciscans. I could hardly believe this was happening. We drove down along the coast, then through mountains—saw the gorgeous colors of the trees, saw castles on the peaks of the mountains, saw the river (*fiume*) Salvo rushing along with waterfalls everywhere. We stopped periodically just to listen to the water—no wonder Francis loved this Umbria.

Assisi in the afternoon sunlight

Then we saw Assisi across the valley, pink and beautiful in the setting sun, as we drove along the highway from Perugia—tears streamed down my cheeks. We drove through the Porto de Francisco and up the narrow stone road to the hotel.

After dinner, in the twilight, we walked through the center of town. Rob, Caitlin and Joseph were running on the steep narrow streets—I could imagine St. Francis as a child running through these streets. It was much more meaningful to me having the little ones with me.

We saw a group of local young men sitting at a table on the sidewalk outside a tavern, drinking wine and being very noisy just like Francis did as a young man.

From the courtyard of the church, we looked out over the town—a half moon and the evening star were shining in the western sky. Later in the hotel room, the windows were open, bright geraniums in the window box framed the open windows. I listened to people talking and men singing in the street below.

The next day, I went to the 7:00 a.m. Mass in the upper part of the basilica, then walked down to the tomb of St. Francis in the lower part, to say the Liturgy of the Hours. A Mass was just starting there—at least twenty-five Franciscan priests were present. Many nationalities were represented—black, brown, yellow, white.

We didn't have enough time to visit all the places in Assisi—I chose to visit Francis' cells on Mt. Subasio—I was so glad I did. There were less people there and you must be quiet. The mountain is rugged with deep gorges where the tiny cells Francis and his followers used for prayer were located. They must have been much smaller in stature than I, for I stooped and barely made it through the door.

It was a beautiful, quiet walk down the forest path to the altar where St. Francis preached to the birds—I said the Crown Rosary walking there. I asked St. Francis to let me make it through that walk—it was miraculous that my knee held out through it all (that was before my knee replacement). In fact, I didn't even feel tired—a wonderful experience. I felt that Francis was with me.

We finished off the day by driving all the way to the top of the mountain, up above the tree line. From there we looked out over Francis' world as a cold chilling rain fell. What a wonderful day! What a wonderful weekend!

Then it was time to go back to the States. Bob drove me to Milan for the return flight. On board the plane, I said to the gentleman alongside me: "I wonder why they switched from the 747 to this smaller plane."

He stared at me and said: "Have you been here in Italy since United was flying the 747s here? You must really be wealthy to afford staying here that long."

"My son and his family live here."

"Okay, that explains it."

****

The '80s and '90s also brought sorrow and changes in the family which I feel I should share with you. Sean and Dotty's twin girls, Kelly and Erin, were born prematurely March 21, 1984. They were so tiny Sean could have fit them into his hand. For the next three months, we visited them in the hospital, watching them growing and gaining weight. We rejoiced the day we heard their first cry.

Sean and Dotty brought the girls home right before their due date. It was a bittersweet day for them—they were told that day that Kelly was blind and Erin had suffered a major brain bleed. Mom and Dad kept a very positive attitude though and learned how to deal with the new developments.

At that time, Sean was working for Beech Aerospace at Ft. Huachuca, Arizona. A few months later, the company told him there was an opening in Spain if he wanted it. They decided to "go for it" even though Sean was needed at the position immediately. Dotty stayed behind so the girls, then five months, weighing seven pounds, could receive a complete physical checkup before leaving. I was with her the morning of the appointment. As the doctor finished up, she said: "I'm sorry to tell you that Kelly has cerebral palsy and possibly will never walk."

With all the papers and documents in hand we left the office. Dotty kept her positive attitude and made the final arrangements for their flight to Spain. I told her I'd go with her to help on the flight—she didn't want me to do that and off she went with the girls. She found friendly people on the planes. They held one of the girls for her during take-offs and landings.

She said she'll never forget the look on the doctor's face as she handed him all the paperwork for the twins on her first visit to him upon their arrival in Spain. However, he became a good friend of the family and often had dinner with them during the fifteen months they lived there.

They came back to the States when the girls needed more specialized medical help—Kelly needed eye surgery. Sean worked at the BASI office in Tampa, Florida, upon their return. Their son, Ryan, was born there.

Kelly and Erin are beautiful young ladies of twenty-four years now—Kelly is blind and, despite the cerebral palsy, walks very well with the aid of braces; Erin has sight after operations to retain the retina.

Our son Hilary competed in cross-country running during his high school and college years. As we talked about this part of the book, he recalled what he did for his nieces and nephew during that time—I asked him to write about it. This is what he wrote about Kelly.

Hilary

My first of three runs of prayer begins in Yuma, Arizona, at a road race. I believe it was February of 1986 when I ran the race for my niece, Kelly, who was to have surgery on her eye. All that I did in that race was to be offered up for her successful operation.

The race started as most do, with a pack of runners. My friend Dan and I were in the front pack, but the focus and the talk seemed to be on an individual who was local and sponsored by a shoe company.

As we neared the halfway point, the pack had narrowed to me, Dan and the race favorite. (The race pace was between 5 minute to 5:30 pace.) As the battle raged among the three of us, I did something that does not often happen in a race. I was about to go into a spiritual level of running.

I was thinking about what I needed to do: to throw in a surge where we did a turn at the halfway point. I was hurting but the thought of Kelly and what she was going through reminded me this was for her, not for me. This was to give her strength: not for me to win a race.

I put in a surge on the first turn and the favored runner responded, while Dan went out the back. The second turn had a small uphill; I knew if I was going to do this for Kelly, I needed to surge off of the first surge to break the favored runner. Even though I was in pain, I knew I had to do it for Kelly. These thoughts were more of an offering of pain at the spiritual level than at a cognitive level. These runs of Grace cannot be conquered at a physical level, but the great physical shape is needed to withstand them.

I went on to win the race and received a large silver urn as a trophy. After returning to Tucson, I mailed the urn to Kelly—it was her victory through God's intervention.

Several years later, I was talking to my friend, Bo Reed—he mentioned the name of that favored runner. I told him I won the race with him in 1986. Bo looked at me and said that at that time no one could touch him in a race. He was one of the top runners at the university level and the best runner in Arizona at the time. It was then that I fully realized how spiritual that run was that day in Yuma. There was no way I could have beaten him at a physical level.

****

Our son Cronan and his wife, Tina, live in the Quad Cities. In 1982, their son, David, who was fourteen months old at the time, was diagnosed as clinically deaf—they started communicating with him in sign language. Two years later, he had trouble with his eyesight: doctors discovered cataracts on both of his eyes. These were removed and they hoped the major problems were solved.

In 1986, when their youngest child, Mary, was two months old, physicians discovered she had two holes in her heart; in addition, she had a valve blockage between the heart and lungs. Corrective surgery was performed and the results were satisfactory. She also was diagnosed as clinically deaf.

Between 1987 and 1988, cataracts developed in both of her eyes and were surgically removed. Also in 1987, David experienced difficulty in chewing his food. Medical officials postulated a possible tumor or stroke and referred him to Children's Hospital in Iowa City where extensive tests were conducted for almost a year. Hospital officials finally felt they isolated the medical problem to progressive bulbar palsy, a neuromuscular disease which deteriorates all muscle coordination in the body, starting at the mouth and working its way down.

While they were performing tests on David, muscular degeneration developed affecting his neck and legs—he was fitted with leg braces. The degeneration continued and by 1989, he was confined to a wheelchair. Neck muscular capabilities kept deteriorating and a tube was surgically implanted in his stomach so he could receive a liquid diet. The leg muscle deterioration caused frequent muscle spasms so medication was prescribed to relieve the pain.

At Thanksgiving time in 1989, Mary's medical state began to deteriorate. By January, she was confined to a wheelchair and further tests conducted at the University of Iowa Hospitals disproved that both children had bulbar palsy. They now concluded that David and Mary had a rare neurological muscular disorder which has no name or cure. They determined this because palsy does not involve deafness, cataracts or muscle spasms.

Mary continued to decline—in June of 1990, a tube was surgically implanted to accommodate a liquid diet. She began having muscle spasms and her pain was controlled by various medications. Later she was placed on oxygen and prescribed medication to try to alleviate the pain.

During all this time, Cronan and Tina showed their deep love for their children by keeping David and Mary in the home, learning how to administer the prescribed medication and liquid diets for them—two rooms looked like hospital rooms. They wanted David and Mary to stay part of the family which included the oldest son, Louis, their daughter Christina and another son, Patrick. All of them learned sign language and communicated well with David and Mary.

(Christina is now the teacher for the deaf, pre-kindergarten through twelfth grade, in the Houston, Missouri, School District.)

Their attitude was really good. A counselor, George McDoniel, the director of Easter Seals for the Quad Cities, became a very good friend of David—he could use sign language and helped David with his counseling.

Family inspiration came from a strong belief in God and in each other. They had hope and faith in God and the hope that a miracle will occur, but if not, there's always heaven.

Their strength also came from the outpouring of help from neighbors, friends and parishioners of St. Patrick Church in Colona, Illinois—Stephanie Dowdal, one of the parishioners, organized a fund raiser to help with the expenses of a visiting nurse during the evening hours as the children needed extensive medical attention all the time.

Mary and David also inspired them—their smiles, even in their pain, gave Mom and Dad and the other children the strength to smile.

I went there at times to be with the other children when Mom and Dad had to be with Mary and David at the hospital. During those times, I witnessed the intense pain Mary and David endured and the sufferings of Mom and Dad as they held the children to soothe them.

Mary died on February 27, 1991, when she was five years old; David died September 12, 1993, when he was twelve years old. Tina and Cronan had beautiful mementos of their lives in the funeral home. Cronan's poem in memory of David and was part of that.

David
What a Life!

He was never able to hear a bird sing
or hear the sound of jazz
He never heard his mother call
or was able to call his Mom
What a Life!

He lost his ability to chew at seven
lost his ability to walk at eight.
What a Life!

He lost his little sister of the same
disease when only age ten.
He witnessed the grueling torture she endured
and knew he would endure the same.
What a Life!

He lay in bed and watched TV.
remembered all the fun.
He learned to say the rosary
He prayed it every day.
God only knows how many lives he touched
or even how many he saved.

For he prayed for friends and relatives
and kept a cheerful smile.
What a life he has led!
an example for us all.

Dad

Hilary wrote this about Mary and David.

Hilary

This second run was not a race as we know them to be on Earth, but rather a run reaching from the bounds of Earth to those of Heaven. It was February 28, 1991, the day after the death of my niece, Mary; I drove my white Camaro up to Shultz Pass Road in Flagstaff, Arizona. It was the beginning of a thirty-inch snowstorm and there was about a foot of snow on the ground already.

As I stretched and warmed up for the run, I began the process of praying and offering this run up to Mary. There was no set prayer, just the contemplation of how her disease had not given her the opportunity to run through the beauty of Earth.

The run began up a forest path that followed a stream beside the forest road. All was covered with snow and this wet snow was hanging heavy upon the Ponderosa Pine. Upon my shoulders, was the giggling, hair bouncing presence of Mary. She had been unable to travel freely within the forests of this world when she was alive, yet now she had shed this restraint and I was the avenue in which she would travel.

After running a mile or two with her upon my shoulder, I let Mary know that she had been along for this ride, now it was time for her to take the controls. These well-tuned legs and arms, these deep-breathing lungs, and this strong throbbing heart were hers to use. She melted into the boundary of my skin and led me on up the mountain trail that turned into a two-rut hunting road. Up we went to the open meadow filled with near knee-deep snow and skirted the left side of a small pond. Still the giant flakes fluttered down from the gray sky. She pushed me on, not backing off the pace, unhampered from her previous ailments. The steepness of the mountain made no matter and the depth of the snow were of no consequence.

Sometimes I would waver, like those times in prayer when we let go of God but then reclaim our focus. We came weaving down the switch-back trail on the other side of the meadow until we reached a road that led back to the car. Mary remained with me as we cruised down the road. She had seen the mountains on the stride of legs that she controlled upon this precious gift of a planet. With a grand smile and a giggle, she left me to be in her new freedom of eternity.

As I reflect on this time with Mary, I wonder if my ability to run had not been for what I achieved in high school and at the university level. Those times may have only prepared me for this gift of running with Mary and later with her brother. The purity and whiteness of that snow showed me that the suffering that Mary went through in life had truly fulfilled what John saw when he wrote this line in Revelations "...they have washed their robes and made them white in the blood of the Lamb" (Re.7:14).

This final run was not done alone, but with my good friend, Bo Reed. On September 13, 1993, we planned on doing a run in the morning for my nephew, David, who had died the previous day. Bo had come to know and admire the greatness of David and his sister, Mary. I had talked to Bo about my run with Mary and, along with our friend Milfred Tewawina; we had spent countless hours discussing the connection of faith in running. Milfred is Hopi and had given Bo and myself a greater understanding of the connection of prayer with the running and with the creatures of the Earth. Please excuse my long introduction, but there is a reason for it.

As usual, it was a breezy day in Flagstaff as Bo and I started our run up toward Buffalo Park. I was going to rely a lot on Bo because I was out of shape due to a recent injury, so total length of the run was only about five miles. When we reached the park, I was struggling to keep up and to get into a prayerful state. Then Bo said: "Hill's, look up—he's here." I looked up and saw a red-tailed hawk glide across the park. With that, all pain went away and we shifted up to a new pace. God knew that I could not physically handle a run with David, so he let him be with us in prayer through the presence of a hawk. As we finished our trip around the park, we thanked God for our time with David and then the hawk was gone. We continued our mile-run back to the apartment without saying much; I was struggling again by the time we reached the end of the run. After we stopped, Bo looked at me and said: "The wind has stopped." For that short moment at the end of the run, the wind had stopped as if to say "Amen" and then started to blow again.

I had always wanted to get in shape again to go on a run with David like I did with Mary, but a foot injury ended my running. Bo has only seen that hawk at Buffalo Park one other time since that run and it was on the day of David's funeral.

During the time following David's death, Cronan often looked through the scrapbooks Tina had lovingly made during Mary and David's lifetimes. One particular evening, as he was looking at some pictures of David, he suddenly realized what David had been struggling to sign to him at the end—now he knew! David signed: "I see the Light!" At that moment, Cronan felt David's hand on his shoulder saying: "Gosh, Dad, I didn't think you'd ever get it!"

****

In August of 1994, I was in Flagstaff with Brigid and Brian's family. I stayed with the other children, Alisha and Aaron, while Mom and Dad took Emile, two and a half years old at the time, for some tests. Brigid noticed a lump on Emile's abdomen one day: the family doctor sent them to Phoenix to get it checked—they returned home to await the results of the test.

I then took the train in Flagstaff to Gallup, New Mexico, to be with our daughter Camille's family when she delivered their new addition to the family—Bethany was born August 29.

A few days later, Brigid called with the sad news that Emile had a Wilmes tumor on one kidney: they were taking her to Phoenix for surgery to remove the kidney.

Terry went to Flagstaff to be with the children until I returned from Gallup on the train. Emile's surgery went well and the prognosis was good. She underwent radiation treatments and chemotherapy for a while after that.

After the initial stay in Flagstaff, I returned home and subsequently stayed at the Ronald McDonald House in Phoenix with the children when Brian and Brigid came there for Emile's regular treatments. She was such a little trooper all the way through—she bounced back after each treatment going full tilt.

One time in particular I remember. The children and I were sitting on the couch near the entrance of the Ronald McDonald House. Emile came running through the front door with her mom and dad—she was still a little unsteady from the anesthesia the treatment required but she was determined to get to that play room that she loved. I cried as I watched her—that determination got her through her ordeal. Now, she's a young lady, sixteen years old and still going strong.

****

In 1993, Bob, Nancy, Rob, Caitlin and Joseph returned to the States after their stay in Italy where Bob worked for BASI. They rented a house two doors down from us. Nancy was pregnant with twins at the time.

Twin girls, Gillian and Maegan, were born in September while we were in the Quad Cities for our grandson David's funeral.

In 1995, Gillian, at age two, was diagnosed with acute lymphatic leukemia, commonly known as cancer of the blood. She started on the appropriate chemotherapy protocol. This treatment continued for two years with clinic visits every week, some with hospitalization. I stayed with the other children when Nancy was with Gillian.

By the end of 1997, the prospects for Gillian were favorable enough for the family to move to Holbrook, a small city about 376 miles northeast of Tucson. Shortly after the move, Maegan's health began to decline. It took three bone marrow tests to reach the same diagnosis as Gillian's. In April of 1998, the 752-mile round trip to Tucson was necessary for the aggressive treatment to be initiated.

Through a friend of the family, Sister Carolyn, Nancy learned about Angel Flight missions—Sr. Carolyn knew a pilot, Frank Niehaus, who had a small plane and was part of that group who volunteered to fly patients needing medical treatment. Frank along with Buck Hellickson (a friend of the family in Holbrook, who also had a small plane) indeed were angels to us—I flew with them from Tucson to Holbrook to be with the rest of the family there—Nancy and Maegan took the plane back to Tucson to be at the hospital there. We made many flights—the flight over the White Mountains became very familiar to us.

One flight I made with Frank I remember well. Strong winds in Holbrook delayed our return flight to Tucson. We started off at sunset—the view across the desert as the sun was setting was awesome. I couldn't take my eyes off it. Then Frank tapped me on the shoulder and pointed to the east on his side of the plane. A full moon was reflected on San Carlos Lake—what beauty God lavishes on us!

Gillian and Maegan are young ladies of fourteen years now.

We witnessed again and again during these years that a family's love can absorb much hurt and sorrow and cushion it to make it bearable.

Chapter XII

And Beyond

It's been a while since I mentioned anything about a flight in a Stearman. I had not completely forgotten about wanting that flight but as the years passed the memory of the Stearman faded.

Then in May of 2004, I read a book by Stephen Coonts entitled *Cannibal Queen*: the story of his adventures flying this Stearman to all of the forty-eight states. That did it—I wanted that ride in a Stearman!

Stephen wrote about taking people for rides as he flew through the States. I called the library to get his current address—he was close by in Las Vegas; I could easily get there.

I wrote a letter to him and received an answer within a week. But no luck: he sold the Stearman and bought one with an enclosed cockpit and two engines. Foiled again!

A few months later, I talked about my dilemma with our son, Cronan: he's part of team maintaining the corporate jets for John Deere Company in Moline, Illinois. He knew a pilot who just bought a Stearman: he said he'd talk to him about taking me for a ride when we were in the area for our grandson's wedding. No such luck—Cronan said the pilot didn't feel comfortable enough flying the Stearman to take me up: he felt he needed more flying time in that type of plane. Foiled again!

A year later, Cronan sent us an email he received from that pilot after he asked about him taking me up when Terry and I were in that area again for our fifty-fifth wedding anniversary reunion.

Cronan: sounds good. The Stearman is on the grass strip in Geneseo, so we would probably fly out of there. That is the weekend of the Quad

*Cities air show so you might think about taking her to that one day too.
Sounds like she might enjoy it! PS. If you really want to get her excited,
send her a picture of the Stearman! It's a beautiful airplane. Totally
restored in 2000.*

Wow, I could hardly wait!

Terry and I arrived in St. Louis and rented a car to our final destination at
Eagle Hurst Ranch in Steelville, Missouri, where the reunion was held. The
host family, our son Rory his wife Amy and daughters Cara and Alanna,
greeted us: the whole place had been rented for five days for our fifty-fifth
wedding anniversary reunion. Cara had the cabins mapped out for each of the
families; tee shirts with the family logo and designated colors for the families
were given out. All ten of our children and thirty-seven of our forty-two
grandchildren came at different intervals: from Oregon, California, Arizona,
Illinois and North Dakota and grandchildren from Washington, Texas and
Illinois. Terry's brother-in-law from Michigan and his brother and wife from
Massachusetts, Terry's former student Rosie and his daughter from Suriname,
South America, two of my sisters from Missouri and Fr. Benet Fonck, O.F.M.,
from St. Louis, who celebrated our anniversary Mass, also took part in the
celebration. It was truly awesome!

At the end of the week, when all the final good-byes were said, Terry and
I drove to the Quad Cities for my Stearman flight. Cronan emailed beforehand
the height of the cockpit of the Stearman: I had practiced climbing into
something that high at home: it was the height of our dining room table.

Cronan took us to the hangar at the grass field to look for the pilot: all
attempts to contact the pilot by phone, as previously planned, had failed. The
hangar was empty! The man working in the adjoining hangar said the Stearman
had permanently been moved to the big airport in Davenport. The annual air
show was in progress at that field so flights from there would be impossible;
all attempts to contact the pilot were futile. I don't know who looked the more
devastated—my son or I. Foiled again, but not to worry, I had a contingency
plan.

Our son Chris lives near Portland, Oregon. He was checking on a Beech
Travel Air, a bi-wing, open-cockpit plane (with a door to the cockpit—yes!!)
that provided flights for tourists down the Columbia River Gorge in the
summer—not a Stearman but a pretty good substitute.

The elusive goal of taking a flight in a Stearman drew me ever onward— like the rabbit that coaxes the greyhound down the racetrack. That goal took me from a field in Harbor Springs, Michigan, to a possible flight in the *Cannibal Queen* in Las Vegas, on to a grass field in Moline, Illinois, and now to Portland, Oregon, where Chris scheduled a flight for me on August 20, 2005, at 10:00 a.m. in a Travel Air down the Columbia River Gorge.

Our son Sean, at United Airlines, listed Terry and me as stand-bys on a flight out of Tucson on August 17 to Portland via Los Angeles. We were bumped on the first flight out of Los Angeles but caught the second flight to Portland and were greeted by Chris and family. They thanked us for bringing the sun and warm weather along with us.

The sun stayed with us the following two days—Saturday, the twentieth brought in a coastal flow: a dense fog hanging about fifty feet from the ground. We blamed Sean for bringing it from San Francisco when he flew up Friday morning.

The pilot was waiting for us at 10:00 but pointed to the control tower where the beacon light shone: only IFR flights permitted to fly. They expected the flow to move out by 10:30 when his next flight was scheduled—he had a full schedule after that until the first of the week when we'd be gone.

"Mom, I must confess that I turned down the 11:00 a.m. flight because I thought you would have a smoother flight earlier in the morning at 10:00."

"That's okay, Chris, we'll try again. Sean said they have some Stearman flights later in the year in San Francisco."

Chris went back to talk with the pilot again: he came back with a big smile on his face.

"Jim said he normally only flies until 3:00 p.m. but he'll take you up after his 3:00 flight."

"Yeah, I'll fly today!"

At 3:00 p.m. the whole entourage arrived—Chris' family, Sean, Terry and me replete in Chris' old leather flight jacket with a Snoopy flying scarf around my neck and the helmet and goggles given me by the pilot. (I had to relinquish the jacket and scarf because the pilot said it was too warm up there.) Chris and Sean's video and digital cameras and Terry's trusty Pentax recorded it all.

Jim and Thecla by the Travel-Air

It was a "two-thumbs up" flight all the way—more wonderful than I ever imagined. Jim told me I could hang my head out the side of the cockpit except on take-off and landing when he needed to see where he was going. And hang out I did—I loved the smell of the engine and the feel of the prop blast. Gorgeous scenery greeted us everywhere: the beautiful river, the huge rock sides of the gorge where one of the longest waterfalls anywhere flowed from one side of it: the feel of the plane banking for a better look at it was super. At 1,000 feet, I could wave at the people on the beach on an island in the river. This truly is what flying's all about! Mission accomplished and it was well worth the wait!

After the flight, Jim had me write about myself in his guest book—he was quite taken aback at my age (eighty) and the size of my family. He showed me one of the entries in the book which was from a man traveling through Oregon who saw the ad for the rides and came in to take a ride. He showed Jim a check his grandfather had given him that was made out to Charles Lindberg and endorsed by him for a flight his grandfather made with Lindberg when he was barnstorming across the States.

Jim truly loved his plane: a Travel Air built in 1929 (four years younger than me) by Beech, Cessna and Stearman (the plane was part Stearman)—Cessna and Stearman went their own ways after that. The plane for a time was a crop duster here in the States and then for a time in South America. Jim replaced the original 90-horsepower radial engine with a 300-horsepower radial engine—we traveled at 90mph. He said he could get to 100 or 120 if he really pushed it.

I emailed Stephen Coonts in September of 2005 telling him of my flight in the Travel Air—his return email: "Glad you got that ride! It'll probably be one you'll not forget. Steve Coonts."

Terry and I still travel a lot—Sean keeps busy at United Airlines booking us as stand-bys on trips visiting his family in California, my relatives and our children in Missouri, Illinois, North Dakota and Oregon. We also went to Mother Angelica's Our Lady of the Angels Monastery in Alabama and gave her a copy of my first book.

Even though I travel with a wheelchair now (I wear a brace on my left foot), we get along fine—I can walk pushing the chair with the carry-on bags in it and can sit down when I need to. That gets us through security faster too and since we travel light with our bag in the wheelchair (it goes down below the plane with the wheelchair), the process of going to the baggage claim is eliminated.

When the Four Freshmen singing group held their three-day conference in Portland in August of 2007, we decided to catch that conference—we could stay with Chris and his family in nearby Sandy. (We had many records of the original Four Freshmen, one of which was with the Stan Kenton orchestra.)

We thoroughly enjoyed the weekend. Chris's wife, Gina, is from Honduras and as we talked one evening, I said: "Gina, I never did get to Honduras to meet your family and see the place where Chris worked down there—I always wanted to do that."

"Why don't you and I go down there now—my family always wanted to meet you."

"Mmm, my passport has long since expired but, why not—okay, let's go for it. I'll get another passport."

"I think it'll be best to plan on going in January—it's a little cooler down there then. You'd better get your passport right away—it takes a long time to get them now."

"I'll do that when we get home."

The local post office said I'd need to make an appointment to apply for the passport. It would be a month before I got an appointment—the main post office told me to come on down any day.

When the man at the reception desk there looked at my application, he said: "Come right on in." Taking me by the arm we walked into another office where they were processing the applications.

"This young lady wants a new passport."

I handed them the application and my last passport: within a few minutes I was on my way out with my receipt. It wasn't until I was home that I realized why the man had said "this young lady" when he showed me in—he probably thought: *why is this eighty-two-year-old woman wanting a ten-year passport?*

I left from Tucson, Gina, from Portland January 17: our destination, Houston. Our flights arrived within a half hour of each other but we didn't know the gate numbers—with cell phones we located each other. We spent the night in Houston.

(On the flight from Tucson, I sat beside a man from Turkey who had been at a conference in Tucson. In our conversation he said: "This was my first visit to the Southwest—I work in Washington, D.C. When I saw the tall cactus as I came out of the terminal, I asked a man if the cactus was real. He gave me a shocked look and assured me that it certainly was."

"What made you think that it wasn't?"

"Well, I have seen the desert in Egypt but never saw any cactus there— they say Tucson is in the desert so I was surprised to see that much growth here.")

Friday, the eighteenth, we were on our way to Tegucigalpa, Honduras, a two-and-a-half-hour flight over the Gulf of Mexico across the Yucatan Peninsula and Belize.

On arrival, we stood in line to get through customs. A lady working there saw me with the wheelchair and told us to go to the diplomat line—there were no people in line there. That was cool. Gina decided she'd take me with her the next time she went home.

Her family was waiting for us—an instant crowd! It was wonderful: sisters, brothers-in-law, nieces, nephews, grandchildren waiting with open arms! Grandma was here with Gina.

Everyone congregated at Gina's sister Chaba and her husband Mario's home and what a fiesta it was. The food was delicious and so much of it. One of the little ones, Michelle, presented me with a drawing of flowers and hearts on a note: "To: Grandma From: Michelle With love. (She's in the first grade of a bilingual school—she speaks and writes English well.)

Chaba's house was beautiful—my room had a balcony overlooking the yard below with flowers of every describable color. The patio by the yard was my favorite spot.

Our first trip took us to the center of the old part of the city where the original cathedral and huge open market are located—everything surrounds the cathedral. In it, in a nave to the left of the main altar, the Blessed Sacrament was exposed for perpetual adoration. It was good to see a large number of people praying there.

The open market is so much fun to visit: so many little stalls with so much to see. Mario and the wheelchair were always there at each stop.

Sunday we attended Mass at the church where Chris and Gina went when they lived here—it was just a block from Chaba's house, up a very steep hill. Mario graciously pushed me up in the wheelchair. Later in the day, we visited the graves of Gina's mom and dad—I did meet her mom when she came to the States one time but I always regretted not meeting her dad before he died. The family brings fresh flowers to the graves every Sunday. The graves lie on a hillside in front of the church which overlooks a beautiful valley.

Driving in Tegucigalpa is not for the fainthearted. I sat in the front seat with Mario and got the thrill of a lifetime. He anticipated all the near-misses and never missed a beat—the horn certainly had its work cut out for it.

Monday morning we set out for San Pedro Sula near Puerto Cortes on the Caribbean coast. On the way we crossed the mountain to Comayagua. Driving across the mountain proved equally as thrilling as driving in the city. The drivers have a sixth sense about when to cross the double yellow line and pass on a curve without meeting an oncoming car.

In Comayagua, we saw the airfield where Chris worked for Beech Aerospace—it is a military base so we were not permitted access. We also saw the house where Chris lived and where Gina joined him after they were married. (Chris rode his motorcycle over the mountain on weekends while dating Gina. She pointed out the spot on one of the curves where he almost "bought the farm" on one of the trips.)

In San Pedro Sula, we met Chaba's oldest daughter who manages the Manpower office there—she asked us to pick up her two daughters, Isabella and Ana from school: she and her husband joined us later at the beach house on the coast.

Our next stop was the home of out gracious hostess, the mother-in-law of another niece, Carolina. We spent the next couple of days in their lovely beach house a few miles away—only about five miles from the Guatemala border.

The sun was low in the sky when we arrived: the sunset was absolutely gorgeous. However, when the main switch was flipped to turn on the electricity, nothing happened. The man in the nearby village said the transformer to our side of the beach was blown—they had men working on it.

It was beautiful watching the light fade on the water as we lay in hammocks strung on the patio—never mind that the stove was electric and the menu for the evening meal changed. Candles provided some light in the kitchen. When the cold chicken salad sandwiches were ready, the lights came on. (An animal had been electrocuted in the transformer causing the blackout.)

What a wonderful few days it was. Isabella and Ana and their mother took a day off and spent the first day with us. Again, I was amazed at how well the children spoke, read and wrote English. They too go to a bilingual school. We had a lot of fun talking and singing songs together. In the evening, I was sitting on the bed praying the Liturgy of the Hours when Isabella, nine years old, came in. She sat alongside of me and read the prayers with me—she pronounced all the words perfectly.

We visited other beaches along the coast, sipped coconut milk straight from the coconut, saw beautiful yachts anchored offshore at little villages. The blues and greens of the water changed as the day progressed. At night, we fell asleep to the sound of the surf.

The lights of the busy Port of Cortes glistened the night we watched storm clouds gathering over the Sea. The young ones let the oncoming surf splash over their feet. But then the rain interrupted the fun and sent all of us scurrying back to the cars.

All too soon, it was time to leave and go back across the mountain. We stopped at a restaurant along the way that had huge carvings of people made from what had to be huge trees. It was there that I saw my first oxcart in Honduras—I saw them everywhere when we lived in Costa Rica in the '60s. But this oxcart was different—it had small rubber-tired wheels instead of the beautifully painted wooden wheels of those in Costa Rica.

At a gas station, which looked like any station we see here in the States with the many semi trucks parked around it, men with huge guns patrolled the whole area. I looked into the face of one of them as he walked by the van—the look in his eyes made me shiver. All this security was necessary because of the problem of armed robberies that were prevalent in these areas.

During the next few days we visited museums—Museo Para La Identidad Nacional and at the Fortress of San Fernando de Omoa. Each day, at some time of the day, everyone gathered to eat at one of the relatives' house—such gracious people.

I'm so grateful the opportunity was given me to meet Gina's family—I got to know her better. I saw the home where she was born, the school and university she attended: she later taught there. Her sisters do beautiful crochet, embroidery and bead work. One sister lives in the old part of the city where her daughter, a medical doctor, has her clinic. A niece, Jessica, is a lawyer working in the tourist office of the government, her niece, Carolina and her husband, Fernando, are doctors. Carolina is a dermatologist and has her own office. Fernando is an internal medicine doctor and works in Hospital Escuela.

Tita's husband, Rene, saw a copy of my book and brought me a book, *Gringos In Honduras 'The Good, the Bad, and the Ugly'* written by an author he knows, Guillermo Yuscaran. Among those he writes about are O. Henry and Eugene O'Neill.

Sunday morning we were back at the airport for our return trip. All the family was there to see us off. There weren't very many dry eyes. I was reminded of the conversation I had with the man sitting next to me on the plane when we came. He asked: "Have you ever been to Honduras before?"

"No, this is my first trip. I want to meet my daughter-in-law's family."

His face lit up when I said that.

"That is so kind of you to do that. That's what my life's work is about. Today, I'm bringing ten duffel bags of portraits for the 500 children in an orphanage just outside of Tegucigalpa to help them keep a memory of their childhood. The portraits are done by artists in the States from pictures I took of the children here—the portraits personalize each child with someone."

His name was Ben Schumaker. He is the founder of The Memory Project: inspiring action and compassion on behalf of children around the world. He started the foundation after visiting an orphanage in Guatemala. He was so glad I found a way to get to know Gina's family better.

In Houston, there was an incredibly long line of people waiting to go through Customs—Gina said she had never seen that many before. How was I to get to my connecting flight within one and a half hours? I saw a man directing the long line.

"Sir, is there any chance of my getting through to catch my connecting flight?"

He looked at me and the wheelchair and Gina.

"Follow me."

Off we went to the diplomat line and soon were on our way to the gate for my next flight. The lady who made sure I got my wheelchair when we deplaned was waiting for me outside of customs to steer me in the right direction for my gate.

"I like your spirit traveling the way you do—I'll remember that when I get your age."

"Thank you—I hope there are nice people to help you then like you're helping me now."

I barely made it to my flight for Tucson. Gina was sad to have me go the rest of the way alone. The lady at the gate said she knew I had a wheelchair and had called my name as they started boarding so I would be among the first on board. Now, as I entered the jetway, there was a long line ahead of me. Two young ladies in front of me took my bags out of the wheelchair.

"You sit down and we'll carry the bags—in fact, I think we have someone to push you too."

I turned my head and saw a nice young man standing behind me, ready to push. Talk about service!

Then I was back in Tucson in the arms of Terry—it was good to be home again.

"Are you going to stay put for a while now?"

"Sure…but our granddaughter Sarah will be defending her dissertation for her doctorate at the University of Pennsylvania in Philadelphia this spring. I've never been to anything like that before…"

So my liberated life goes on —I've made many happy landings in many different places so far and look forward to many more. Cardinal O'Malley's statement at the beginning of this book says it all.

Where They Are Now

Terry Jr. attended West Texas State University in Canyon, TX, graduated with a B.S. in agronomy. He and his wife, Sue, lived in Bolivia for a time and now live in Tucson, AZ, where he owns a home maintenance and remodeling business. They have three children, Sarah, Rebekah and Terry III and his wife, Amanda.

Kevin joined the USMC in 1971 and four years later, with the rank of sergeant, rejoined civilian life and earned a two-year degree for diesel engine mechanic. He and his wife, Micki, live in Elmwood, IL, where he works for a company that manufactures specialized attachments on mining and recycling haulage equipment. They have four children, Carmen, Matthew, Nathan, his wife Ellen, and Joshua.

Rory attended the University of Missouri Rolla and graduated in May of 1978 with a B.S. degree in geological engineering. He worked as a mining engineer for Dow Chemical and then as an environmental engineer at Ft. Leonard Wood. He and his wife, Amy, live in Rolla, MO, where he now works with Brewer Science, Inc., a semi-conductor specialty chemical manufacturer, as environmental manager. They have four children, Ben, Cara, Amalie and Alanna.

Bob enrolled at Spartan School of Aeronautics in Tulsa, OK, and received a diploma in aviation electronics. He became a field service representative on C-12 aircraft for Beech Aerospace Services, Inc., and moved to Athens, Greece, covering C-12 electronics maintenance primarily in the Middle East for BASI and with additional travel to Africa, Europe, Southeast Asia and Australia for them. He, his wife Nancy and family lived in Vicenza, Italy, for two and a half years and now live in Holbrook, AZ, with their children, Rob, Caitlin, Joseph, twins, Gillian and Maegan, Stacey and Abigail.

Cronan attended Spartan School of Aeronautics and obtained an associate degree in applied science with an airframe and powerplant license. He and his wife, Tina, now live in Colona, IL. He works as an aircraft maintenance technician on the corporate aircraft for John Deere Company in Moline. They have five children, Louis, his wife Stephanie and children, Adam and Julia, Christina, David, who died at age twelve of a rare genetic disorder, Patrick, and Mary, who also died at the age of five of the rare genetic disorder.

Sean attended Texas State Technical College in Waco, TX, and obtained an aviation maintenance and airframe license. He and his family moved to Spain for a few years where he worked for Beech Aerospace Services, Inc. He, his wife, Dotty, twins, Kelly and Erin, and Ryan now live in Vacaville, CA. He works in maintenance control on engines at United Airlines in San Francisco, CA.

Chris attended Spartan School of Aeronautics and obtained an aviation maintenance technician license. He worked in Germany for four years and then in Honduras for two years where he met and married his wife, Gina. They now live in Sandy, OR, with their two children, Valentin and Isabella. He recently formed his own corporation, specializing in flying and maintaining Beech King Air aircraft.

Brigid worked for Burr-Brown, a semi-conductor company in Tucson as an engineering technician where she also helped an employee with experiments done for a doctorate program. She met her husband, Brian Kram, there. They now live in Catalina, AZ, with their children, Alisha, Emile, Aaron, Miriam, Kolbe, Aidan and Agnes. She is a full-time mother and home-school teacher.

Hilary graduated from Northern Arizona University with a B.S. in history with a minor in earth science. He has a secondary education certification for seventh through twelfth grades and English as a Second Language (ESL) endorsement. He competed in long-distance running in high school and college years and is still listed in the top ten runners at Pima Community College. He and his wife, Laura, live in Glendale, AZ, with their children, Trevor and Aine, where he teaches at Apollo School and is head coach for the cross country team.

Camille attended Northern Arizona University and earned a bachelor's degree with a major in special education. She taught language arts and reading at a middle school in Gallup, NM, where she met her husband, Duane Smith. They now live in Fargo, ND, with their children, Hannah, Bethany, Veronica, Lydia and Colette. She is a stay-at-home mom and a home educator of their daughters.

All of our children pursued their higher education on their own.

LaVergne, TN USA
14 September 2009
157883LV00004B/186/P